Growth Hacking: How it helps you get new customers and keep existing.

Tomasz Dmuchowski

Warsaw 2023

Growth Hacking: How it helps you get new customers and keep
existing ones

Editing: Tomasz Dmuchowski
Correction: Tomasz Dmuchowski

Copyright © Tomasz Dmuchowski

1st edition
Warsaw 2023

Composition and breaking:
Jakub Dmuchowski

Disclaimer: This
publication has been prepared with due care to provide
accurate and reliable facts.

ISBN 9798392223473

Chapter 1: What is Growth Hacking?

In today's dynamic marketing world, where competition is fierce and new technologies are constantly changing the rules of the game, Growth Hacking is gaining more and more recognition as an effective strategy for companies striving for rapid growth. In this chapter, we'll take a look at what Growth Hacking actually is, what its goals are, and how it differs from traditional marketing strategies.

1.1. Definition of Growth Hacking

Growth Hacking is an innovative marketing strategy whose main goal is to achieve rapid growth of the company by increasing the number of customers, revenues or brand recognition. Unlike traditional marketing strategies, it relies on the creative use of technology, data and experimentation to acquire, maintain and grow a customer base.

The term "Growth Hacking" was first used by Sean Ellis in 2010. Ellis, being an entrepreneur, marketer and consultant, noticed that many companies achieve success in the market by using unusual, innovative marketing methods and striving to constantly optimize their activities.

1.2. Growth Hacking Goals

The primary goal of Growth Hacking is the rapid growth of the company. It is achieved through the implementation of a number of cooperating objectives, such as:

Acquiring new customers: Growth Hacking aims to attract as many potential customers as possible, some of which will be converted into paid users of the services or products that the company offers.

Customer retention: Growth Hacking strategies are designed to build long-term customer relationships, which translates into increased Customer Lifetime Value (CLV) and reduced ChurnRate customer churn.

Development and reactivation of customers: by introducing new products, services or functions as well as customer segmentation, Growth Hacking focuses on increasing customer engagement and loyalty.

1.3. Growth Hacking and traditional marke=ng

While Growth Hacking uses some elements of traditional marketing, there are several significant differences between these strategies:

Focus on data: Growth Hacking bases its activities on data analysis, which allows for quick decision making and optimization.

Experimentation: Growth Hackers are constantly testing different approaches, tools and tactics to find the most effective methods to achieve their goals. They often use A/B testing techniques that allow you to compare two different versions of the same element (e.g. website or email) and choose the one that brings better results.

Creativity: Growth Hacking is very creative in applying new technologies and innovative marketing methods.
Growth Hackers are not afraid to experiment and look for new solutions, even if they have not yet been tested by the competition.

Flexibility: Growth Hacking is a very flexible strategy that can quickly adapt to changing market conditions. It is not tied to specific time frames or budgets, which allows you to quickly respond to changes and take advantage of new opportunities.

Scalability: Unlike traditional marketing, which often requires a significant increase in budgets as the number of customers increases, Growth Hacking focuses on scalable solutions. Thanks to this, even with limited resources, you can achieve significant growth of the company.

1.4. Growth Hacking Components

In practice, Growth Hacking involves a variety of techniques, tools and communication channels that can be used to achieve growth goals. Some of them are:

Optimization of websites (Conversion Rate Optimization, CRO): it consists in modifying elements of the website, such as headers, colors, layout or content, to increase the number of users who perform the desired actions (e.g. purchase of a product, registration for a newsletter or filling out the contact form and other possibilities).

Viral marketing: is based on encouraging users to share the company's content, products or services among their friends and family, which leads to a rapid increase in brand reach.

The use of social media: it consists in building an engaged community around the brand and creating content that will be willingly shared by users and recommended further.

Lead Generation: Growth Hackers develop strategies to attract leads and collect their contact information to enable further communication and eventual closing of the sale.

Email marketing: using emails to maintain customer relationships, promote new products and services, and reactivate inactive users. Effective e-mail campaigns can significantly increase the number of customers and the company's revenues.

Content marketing: creating valuable and engaging content (e.g. articles, blogs, e-books, videos) that attract potential customers, build brand authority in industry and affect search engine positioning.

Search Engine Optimization (SEO): Practices to increase the visibility of a website in organic search results, leading to more website traffic and, as a result, more customers.

Cooperation with influencers: establishing partnerships with people with a large reach and authority in their niche, which allows you to promote products or services among their large and engaged community.

Marketing automation: using technology to automate repetitive marketing tasks, such as sending emails, managing advertising campaigns, and analyzing data, which saves time and increases efficiency.

Growth Hacking is a modern marketing strategy that focuses on achieving rapid business growth through the creative use of technology, data and experimentation.
Thanks to its flexibility, scalability and emphasis on continuous optimization of operations, Growth Hacking is becoming more and more popular among companies that want to stand out on the market and achieve success. In the following chapters of this book, we will discuss specific techniques and tools that will allow you to implement Growth Hacking in your business.

Chapter 2: Basics of Growth Hacking

In the previous chapter, we discussed what Growth Hacking is and how it differs from traditional marketing strategies. Now it's time to understand the basics of this method and learn how to put it into practice. In this chapter, we will focus on the key elements of Growth Hacking, such as the growth process, metrics, experiments, and data analysis.

2.1. The growth process in Growth Hacking

Success in Growth Hacking is based on strict adherence to the growth process, which consists of the following steps:

1. Defining Growth Goals: At the very beginning, you need to define what goals you want to achieve with Growth Hacking. Examples of growth goals might include increasing the number of users, increasing revenue, or improving customer engagement.

2. Identification of key indicators (KPIs): After defining the goals, you need to choose the right metrics that will allow you to monitor progress and measure the effectiveness of actions. KPIs can include conversion, user reactivation, churn rate, and customer lifetime value.

3. Generating Experiment Ideas: To meet your growth goals, you need to come up with ideas for experiments that can help you meet those goals. Ideas can be in different areas such as

website, email marketing, social media or
SEO.

4. Prioritizing and Scheduling Experiments: Once the
ideas have been generated, it's time to organize
them. Evaluate each idea for its potential impact on growth
goals, costs, risks and time needed to implement it.
Based on this, set priorities and develop an action
plan.

5. Conducting the experiments: Then proceed with the
experiments as planned. Make sure that experiments are
performed according to established procedures
and are properly monitored.

6. Analysis of Results and Optimization: After
completing the experiments, analyze the collected
data and decide which activities have produced the desired results.
Based on these conclusions, optimize your activities and
plan further experiments.

2.2. Key metrics and data analysis

In Growth Hacking, data analysis is a key element that allows you
to assess the effectiveness of actions, identify areas for
improvement and make informed decisions. Here are some
of the most important metrics you should track in your activities:

Number of new users: The number of people using your product or service for the first time.

Conversion Rate: The percentage of users who complete the desired action, such as a purchase, signup, or form completion.

Customer lifetime value (CLV): The expected revenue that the customer generates for the company over the life of the relationship.

Churn rate: The percentage of customers who drop out of your product or service within a certain period of time.

Cost per Customer Acquisition (CAC): The total cost per customer acquisition, including marketing, sales, and other expenses.

Data analysis requires the right tools that will allow you to collect, process and analyze information in an effective and easy to understand way. Some of the popular analytics tools are Google Analytics, Mixpanel, Amplitude and Heap.

2.3. Experimentation and A/B testing

Experimentation is at the heart of Growth Hacking and allows you to continuously optimize your actions to achieve better results. One of the most popular ways to conduct experiments is A/B testing, which involves comparing two different versions of the same item to see which one performs better.

A/B testing can be applied to many areas, such as website optimization, email marketing, online advertising, and social media. There are many tools that make it easier to conduct A/B tests, such as Optimizely, VWO or Google Optimize.

2.4. Learning and iteration

Growth Hacking is a continuous process that is based on a cycle of learning and iteration. After completing the experiments and analyzing the results, it is important to draw conclusions and apply them in the next activities. If an experiment has produced positive results, it is worth scaling it up and implementing it on a larger scale. If, on the other hand, the experiment was not successful, it is worth understanding the reasons for the failure and proceeding with further attempts with an improved approach.

It is important not to be discouraged by failures - in Growth Hacking, every experiment, even a failed one, provides valuable information that helps in the further development of the strategy. The key to success is to maintain a cycle of trials, analysis of results and optimization, which will allow you to constantly improve your marketing activities.

2.5. Growth Hacking culture in the organization

To realize the full potential of Growth Hacking, it is important to introduce its culture to the entire organization. This means that all team members - from the board, through marketing, sales, to product development - should be involved in growth process and jointly strive to achieve the set goals.

The culture of Growth Hacking in an organization can be promoted by:

Regular training and workshops to help teams understand and apply the principles of Growth Hacking in their daily work.

Establishing clear growth goals and KPIs that will be shared by the entire team and monitored regularly.

Introducing a data-driven decision-making process that encourages experimentation, analysis of results, and decision-making based on real-world information.

Establishment of interdisciplinary growth-focused teams that combine different skills and knowledge to create holistic growth strategies.

The fundamentals of Growth Hacking include both understanding the growth process and key elements such as metrics, experimentation, data analytics, and organizational culture. Putting these principles into practice will allow you to achieve your growth goals more effectively, optimize your activities and make your company more competitive on the market. In the following chapters of this book, we'll look at specific Growth Hacking techniques and tools to help you put these fundamentals into practice

2.6 History and Evolution of Growth Hacking

In this chapter, we will discover together the history and evolution of Growth Hacking - an extraordinary marketing strategy that has won the hearts and minds of entrepreneurs around the world. Let's take a short journey through time together to understand where Growth Hacking came from and how it has evolved to this day!

The extraordinary history of Growth Hacking begins at the beginning of the 21st century, when the Internet and new technologies began to rapidly change the market. Traditional marketing was becoming less and less effective, and companies began to look for new, creative ways to reach customers. That's when Growth Hacking was born - as a response to these challenges, combining creativity, analytics and technology.

Sean Ellis, the pioneer of Growth Hacking and founder of GrowthHackers.com, is widely credited with coining the concept. In 2010, he published an article in which he used the term "Growth Hacker" for the first time. Since then, the concept has gained immense popularity and Ellis has become one of the most recognizable faces of this strategy.

Growth Hacking is based on the fundamental idea that every marketing activity should serve one purpose - growth. Customer growth, revenue growth, reach growth – all this is at the heart of the Growth Hacking strategy.
Unlike traditional marketing strategies, Growth Hacking focuses on quickly testing, measuring and optimizing activities, which allows companies to achieve surprising results in a short time.

Over the last several years, Growth Hacking has evolved and changed, adapting to new technologies and market needs. Today, it is an extremely diverse strategy, involving various techniques such as website optimization, lead generation, viral marketing, and the use of social media. All this makes Growth Hacking extremely flexible and able to meet various market challenges.

Success stories of Growth Hacking can be found in the history of many well-known companies. Dropbox, Airbnb, Uber, Tinder – these are just some of them. All these companies have used innovative growth strategies that have allowed them to gain millions of users around the world and become giants in their industries. These inspiring stories show how powerful Growth Hacking can be when used properly.

Growth Hacking is also extremely democratic – it doesn't require huge budgets or huge marketing teams. This is why it has become so popular with start-ups and small businesses that often struggle with limited resources. Thanks to its flexibility and focus on quick experimentation, Growth Hacking allows for an equal fight with large corporations, even if we have a much smaller budget.

In recent years, Growth Hacking has also gained recognition among scientists and experts. There are many books, scientific articles and courses devoted to this strategy.
Today we are witnessing the constant development of tools and techniques related to Growth Hacking, and many companies

consistently invests in the development of its own Growth Hacker teams.

Growth Hacking has shown that in today's world full of technology, creativity and innovation, it is possible to achieve success even with limited resources. In the following chapters of this book, we will delve into specific Growth Hacking techniques and strategies to show you how you too can apply this amazing strategy to your own business!

Chapter 3: Key principles of Growth Hacking

In previous chapters, we covered the basics of Growth Hacking, such as the growth process, metrics, and experimentation. Now is the time to understand the key principles that guide this strategy and lay the foundation for success in the field of growth. In this chapter, we will look at the seven key principles of Growth Hacking.

3.1. Focus on growth goals

Growth Hacking is always focused on achieving specific growth goals, such as increasing the number of users, revenue or engagement. It is important that these goals are clearly defined and measurable so that progress can be monitored and effectiveness assessed.

3.2. Data orientation

Data plays a key role in Growth Hacking as it allows you to make informed decisions, analyze experiment results, and continuously optimize your operations. The principle of data orientation means that all decisions and actions taken as part of the growth strategy should be based on real, objective data.

3.3. Experimentation and iteration

Growth Hacking involves constantly conducting experiments, analyzing their results and implementing improvements based on these observations. Thanks to this approach, it is possible to optimize growth strategies, identify the most effective activities and scale them on a larger scale.

3.4. Creativity and innovation

Growth Hacker must be creative and open to innovative ideas that will allow to stand out on the market and gain new customers more effectively. Creativity can manifest itself both in the approach to problems and in the use of unusual tools or marketing techniques.

3.5. Speed and flexibility

Growth Hacking involves operating with great speed and flexibility. The Growth Hacker must be ready to react quickly to changing market conditions, adapt its strategies and experiment with different solutions to find the most effective ones.

3.6. Scalability

One of the main goals of Growth Hacking is to achieve rapid growth, which requires the implementation of strategies that are scalable and can be applied to various areas of the company's operations. Scalability means the ability to extend and replicate effective marketing activities on a larger scale, with minimal increase in costs.

3.7. Collaboration and communication

Growth Hacking is not the domain of only one department or specialist. In order to achieve optimal results, it is necessary to involve various departments, such as marketing, sales, product development and IT. Collaboration and communication between teams allows for a holistic approach to growth strategy that takes into account diverse perspectives and skills.

In practice, the key principles of Growth Hacking are closely related and complement each other. Focus on growth goals, data orientation, experimentation and creativity are the foundation for developing effective strategies, while speed, flexibility, scalability, as well as cooperation and communication allow for their effective implementation and achievement of the desired results.

In the following chapters of this book, we will look at specific techniques and tools that will allow you to practice apply these key principles of Growth Hacking so that your company can achieve the expected growth.

Chapter 4: Psychology and mechanisms of influence in Growth Hacking

Psychology plays a key role in Growth Hacking, because understanding human behavior, motivation and influence mechanisms allows you to create more effective marketing strategies and activities. In this chapter, we will look at the most important psychological aspects that influence the success of a growth strategy and how to put this knowledge into practice.

4.1. Rules of persuasion

Dr. Robert Cialdini in his book "Influencing People" presented six principles of persuasion that can be effectively used in Growth Hacking. Here they are:

1. The Principle of Reciprocity: People have a natural tendency to repay favors or prejudices received. In Growth Hacking, this principle can be used by offering customers valuable content, free product samples

or special offers to build loyalty and encourage further interaction with the brand.

2. The principle of consistency and consistency: People strive to maintain consistency between their past decisions and current actions. In Growth Hacking, this can be exploited by creating campaigns that build on previous customer commitments, for example through e-mail marketing or remarketing.

3. Principle of sympathy: We are more likely to trust and work with people we like. In Growth Hacking, it is crucial to build a positive brand image that attracts the sympathy of customers, for example by creating friendly and valuable content or being active in social media.

4. Principle of Authority: People are more likely to trust experts and authorities in a given field. In Growth Hacking, this principle can be used by building the brand's image as an expert in its industry, for example by publishing research, articles or speeches at conferences.

5. Principle of Social Approval: People are more likely to make decisions that are in line with what the majority is doing. In Growth Hacking, this can be used by showing customers that many people use a given product or service, for example through numerous opinions, recommendations or the number of followers in social media.

6. Scarcity Principle: Things that are less available or scarce tend to be more valuable. In Growth Hacking, this principle can be exploited by using techniques such as limited-time offers, promotions for first customers or exclusive versions of products that increase the sense of urgency and uniqueness of the offer.

4.2. Anchoring effect

The anchoring effect is that people often base their decisions on the first information they receive, even if that information is not entirely relevant to the situation. In Growth Hacking, you can use the anchoring effect, for example by offering a higher starting price, which will then be lowered as part of a promotion or discount. Customers will compare the new price to the original price, which will make the offer seem more attractive.

4.3. FOMO effect (Fear of Missing Out)

FOMO, or "Fear of Missing Out", is a psychological phenomenon that causes people to strive for what they don't have, fearing that they will regret their decision in the future. Growth Hacking can use FOMO by introducing time-limited promotions, exclusive offers or products available only to selected customers, which increase the sense of urgency and the desire to have a given product or service.

4.4. Halo effect

The halo effect is that people evaluate the whole (e.g. a brand or product) based on one or several features that they consider crucial. In Growth Hacking, you can use the halo effect, ensuring the high quality of all aspects of the brand, such as the appearance of the website, product quality or customer service. Positive experiences in one area can affect the perception of other aspects of the brand.

4.5. Nudging ("push" approach)

Nudging is a strategy based on gently guiding people's behavior through "pushes" (subtle suggestions, changes in the environment or direction of choice) that encourage them to make the desired decisions. Growth Hacking can use nudging, for example, by changing the layout of the website to direct users' attention to key elements, or by using clear calls to action (CTAs) that facilitate purchasing or registration decisions.

Psychology and influence mechanisms are an integral part of Growth Hacking. The use of knowledge about human behavior, motivation and decision-making processes allows for the development of more effective and accurate growth strategies. Proper application of the principles of persuasion, anchoring effects, FOMO, halo and nudging techniques can significantly increase the effectiveness of marketing activities and lead to better results for your company.

In the following chapters of this book, we will look at specific tools and techniques that can be used in practice to strengthen the psychological aspects of Growth Hacking and influence customer behavior more effectively.

Chapter 5: Acquiring new customers - Growth hacking

Acquiring new customers is an important goal for any company, and Growth Hacking offers unique and innovative methods that can strengthen these activities. In this chapter, we will present the key Growth Hacking techniques that will help you acquire new customers more effectively.

5.1. Viral Mark=ng

Viral marketing is a promotion technique that uses contagiousness and the spread of information among users to increase reach and attract new customers. Here are some viral strategies that can be used in Growth Hacking:

- Referral marketing: encouraging customers to refer product or service to friends in exchange for rewards or discounts.

- Contests and giveaways: organizing contests or giving away free products in exchange for participation in the campaign or providing information about the brand.

- Create valuable, engaging and easy shared content (e.g. memes, infographics, videos) that have the potential to go viral.

5.2. Inbound Mark=ng

Inbound marketing is a strategy based on attracting potential customers by creating valuable content and providing them with added value. Growth Hacking can use inbound marketing using the following techniques:

- Content marketing: creation and promotion valuable content that solves the problems and doubts of potential customers and builds trust in the brand.

- SEO (Search Engine Optimization): Optimize your website for search engines to attract more organic traffic.

- Social media marketing: active participation in social media, engaging with users and building a community around the brand.

5.3. Mark=ngu automation

Marketing automation allows you to streamline and scale your marketing activities while minimizing your workload. In Growth Hacking, you can apply automation in various areas, such as:

- E-mail marketing: automation of processes related to sending e-mails, such as welcome campaigns, newsletters and follow-ups.

- Remarketing: automatic display of ads users who have previously visited your website or left contact details.

- Chatbots: the use of artificial intelligence in order customer service automation and lead generation on the website.

5.4. Data analysis and optimization

Data orientation is a key element of Growth Hacking. Data analysis and optimization allows for a better understanding of customer behavior, identifying areas for improvement and making more informed business decisions. Growth Hacking can use data analysis and optimization in various areas:

- A/B testing: running tests on different versions website, advertisements or content to identify which ones deliver better results.

- Web analytics: collecting and analyzing data on website traffic, traffic sources, user behavior or conversions, which allows for optimization of marketing activities.

- User Research: conduct research qualitative, such as interviews or usability tests, to understand the needs, problems and motivations of potential customers.

5.5. Cooperation with partners and networking

Cooperation with other enterprises, organizations or influencers can be an effective way to acquire new customers. Various forms of cooperation can be used in Growth Hacking:

- Strategic partnerships: working with companies that offer complementary products or services, which allows customers to recommend each other.

- Influencer marketing: collaborating with people with a large number of followers on social media that can promote your product or service to their audience.

- Networking and participation in industry events: establishing relationships with other entrepreneurs, potential customers or partners, which can lead to new business opportunities.

Attracting new customers using Growth Hacking involves the use of creative, innovative and effective techniques that help to increase reach, build trust and convert potential customers into loyal consumers. The use of strategies such as viral marketing, inbound marketing, marketing automation, data analysis, optimization and cooperation with partners can significantly increase the effectiveness of marketing activities and lead to an increase in the number of customers.

Chapter 6: Building the Perfect Customer Profile (Buyer Persona)

Creating the perfect customer profile, or Buyer Persona, is a key element in the Growth Hacking process. It allows you to understand the needs, expectations and motivations of potential customers, thanks to which you can better adjust marketing and sales strategies. In this chapter, we will walk you through how to build a Buyer Persona step by step.

6.1. Meaning of Buyer Persona

A Buyer Persona is a fictional representation of your ideal customer, based on real data, market research and analysis. Allows you to:

• Better understanding of customer needs and motivations.

- Adaptation of communication and offer to specific groups of recipients.

- Directing marketing activities to the right target group.

- Increasing the effectiveness of marketing and sales strategies.

6.2. Collecting customer information

To build a Buyer Persona, you need to collect customer information from a variety of sources, such as:

- Demographic data: age, gender, place of residence, education, occupation, income

- Behavioral data: purchasing behavior, preferences, needs, problems that your company solves

- Web analytics: information about users, traffic sources, conversion paths

- Market research: surveys, interviews, discussion groups, competition analysis

6.3. Creating customer segments

On the basis of the collected information, you can create customer segments - groups of recipients with similar characteristics, needs and behaviors. Segmentation allows for a better adjustment of the offer and communication to individual customer groups, which increases the effectiveness of marketing and sales activities.

6.4. Developing a Buyer Persona profile

Based on the collected information and customer segmentation, we can now develop a Buyer Persona profile that includes the following:

- Fictional character's name and description: creating a character makes it easier identification with the recipient and better understanding of his needs

- Demographic information: age, gender, place of residence, education, occupation, income

- Goals and motivations: what goals does the customer want to achieve, what motivates him to buy

- Problems and challenges: what problems does the client face, what challenges do they face

- Communication preferences: how the customer prefers to communicate with the company, what channels and content are most attractive to him

- Purchase path: how the customer gets to your website, what steps he takes before making a purchase, what are they barriers and factors influencing the decision

- Quotes and Testimonials: customer testimonials that reflect them expectations, problems and needs that your company can solve

6.5. Buyer Persona validation and update

Building a Buyer Persona is an iterative process that requires constant validation and updating. It should be checked whether the customer profile corresponds to reality, whether the needs and problems are adequate, and whether the goals and motivations are up to date. This can be done by analyzing data from various sources, conducting market research and talking to customers.

6.6. The use of Buyer Persona in practice

The developed Buyer Persona profile can be used in various aspects of the company's operations, such as:

- Content creation and optimization: adapting content to the needs, problems and motivation of the Buyer Persona, which increases their value and attractiveness to the recipients.

- Planning and implementation of marketing campaigns: directing activities to the right target group, using communication preferences as well as problems and needs of Buyer Persona.

- Optimization of the purchase path: eliminating barriers and factors negatively affecting the decision shopping experience, increasing conversion and customer satisfaction.

- Product development: adapting the offer to the needs,
  expectations and problems of the Buyer Persona, which allows for a
  better understanding of the market and getting ahead of the competition.

Building the perfect customer profile is a key element in the Growth Hacking process. It allows for a better understanding of the needs, expectations and motivations of potential customers, which is necessary for the effective adjustment of marketing, sales and product development strategies. Creating a Buyer Persona is based on collecting information, customer segmentation, developing profiles, validating and updating, as well as the practical use of this information in the company's operations.

Chapter 7: Acquiring new customers - Growth hacking

Acquiring new customers is an important goal for any company, and Growth Hacking offers unique and innovative methods that can strengthen these activities. In this chapter, we will present the key Growth Hacking techniques that will help you acquire new customers more effectively.

7.1. Viral Mark=ng

Viral marketing is a promotion technique that uses contagiousness and the spread of information among users to increase reach and attract new customers. Here are some viral strategies that can be used in Growth Hacking:

- Referral marketing: encouraging customers to refer product or service to friends in exchange for rewards or discounts.

- Contests and giveaways: organizing contests or giving away free products in exchange for participation in the campaign or providing information about the brand.

- Create valuable, engaging and easy shared content (e.g. memes, infographics, videos) that have the potential to go viral.

7.2. Inbound Mark=ng

Inbound marketing is a strategy based on attracting potential customers by creating valuable content and providing them with added value. Growth Hacking can use inbound marketing using the following techniques:

- Content marketing: creation and promotion valuable content that solves the problems and doubts of potential customers and builds trust in the brand.

- SEO (Search Engine Optimization): Optimize your website for search engines to attract more organic traffic.

- Social media marketing: active participation in social media, engaging with users and building a community around the brand.

7.3. Mark=ngu automation

Marketing automation allows you to streamline and scale your marketing activities while minimizing your workload. In Growth Hacking, you can apply automation in various areas, such as:

- E-mail marketing: automation of processes related to sending e-mails, such as welcome campaigns, newsletters and follow-ups.

- Remarketing: automatic display of ads users who have previously visited your website or left contact details.

- Chatbots: the use of artificial intelligence in order customer service automation and lead generation on the website.

7.4. Data analysis and optimization

Data orientation is a key element of Growth Hacking. Data analysis and optimization allows for a better understanding of customer behavior, identifying areas for improvement and making more informed business decisions. IN

Growth Hacking can be used for data analysis and optimization in various fields:

- A/B testing: running tests on different versions website, advertisements or content to identify which ones deliver better results.

- Web analytics: collecting and analyzing data on website traffic, traffic sources, user behavior or conversions, which allows for optimization of marketing activities.

- User Research: conduct research qualitative, such as interviews or usability tests, to understand the needs, problems and motivations of potential customers.

7.5. Cooperation with partners and networking

Cooperation with other enterprises, organizations or influencers can be an effective way to acquire new customers. Various forms of cooperation can be used in Growth Hacking:

- Strategic partnerships: working with companies that offer complementary products or services, which allows customers to recommend each other.

- Influencer marketing: collaborating with people having a large number of followers on social media that can promote your product or service among its audience.

• Networking and participation in industry events: establishing relationships with other entrepreneurs, potential customers or partners, which can lead to new business opportunities.

Chapter 8: Strategies for Getting Traffic to Your Website

Acquiring website traffic is a key aspect in the Growth Hacking process. In this chapter, we will introduce you to various strategies that will help you attract more visitors to your website and increase your chances of conversion.

8.1. Search Engine Optimization (SEO)

SEO (Search Engine Optimization) is a set of activities aimed at improving the positioning of a website in search results. Higher ranking means more visibility and more traffic to your website. The key aspects of SEO are:

- Keyword Selection: Select relevant phrases that are frequently searched by users and are related to your business.

- Content optimization: creating valuable and unique content that is optimized for keywords.

- Link building: gaining valuable links external links leading to your website, which improves your position in search results.

- Technical optimization: taking care of page loading speed, adapting to mobile devices, improving the structure of the page and facilitating indexing by search engine robots.

8.2. content mark=ng

Content marketing is about creating and distributing valuable content that is attractive to your target group and related to your business. The goal of content marketing is to build trust, increase brand awareness and generate website traffic. Content examples:

- Blog articles

- E-books, guides and reports

* Infographics

* Videos and webinars

* Podcasts

8.3. social media mark=ng

The use of social media allows you to increase your reach, build relationships with customers and generate website traffic. Key activities in social media marketing:

* Create compelling content and posts.

* Regular publication and promotion of content.

* Engaging with and responding to users comments.

* Monitoring results and optimizing activities.

8.4. Internet advertising

Online advertising, just like Google Ads or Facebook Ads, allows you to quickly generate traffic to your website. Various types of advertising can be used, such as:

* Search engine text ads

- Display ads on partner sites

- Video advertising on video platforms

- Social media advertising

- Retargeting ads

8.5. Marke=ng e-mail

Email marketing is an effective tool for building customer relationships, promoting content and generating website traffic. Key aspects of email marketing:

- Building a subscriber base: encouraging
  users to subscribe to the newsletter by offering valuable content, promotions or discounts.

- Creating attractive and valuable messages:
  adapting the content to the recipients, maintaining consistency with the brand image.

- Segmentation of the audience list: tailoring messages to specific target groups, which allows for better communication and more effective campaigns.

- Testing and optimization: checking the effectiveness of various elements of the message, such as title, content, CTA or shipping time to optimize the effectiveness of the campaign

8.6. Cooperation with influencers

Cooperation with influencers, i.e. people with a large impact in their industry or target group, can help increase your reach and attract new users to your website.
The key elements of cooperation with influencers are:

- Choosing the right influencers: finding people who have an impact on your target group and are related to your business.

- Establishing relationships with influencers: building relationships, eg by commenting on their content, collaborating in creating content or promoting their activities.

- Creating joint projects: cooperation with influencers in creating valuable content that will be promoted on their channels, e.g. blog entries, videos, podcasts or contests

8.7. Use of viral mark=ng

Viral marketing is the creation and distribution of content that has the potential to spread naturally and quickly among users. Effective viral campaigns generate a lot of website traffic and increase brand awareness. Examples of viral marketing activities include:

- Creating engaging and emotional content:
  valuable and interesting content that people want to share with their friends.

- Using the FOMO effect (Fear of Missing Out):
  creating content that evokes the feeling that it needs to be shared so as not to be left behind.

- Organizing contests and giveaways: initiating activities that motivate users to share content and promote the brand in exchange for prizes.

8.8. Competition analysis

Competition analysis allows you to identify activities that are effective in your industry and understand what can be done better. The key elements of competitor analysis are:

- Collecting information about competitors: identification main competitors, their strategies, content and promotions.

- Monitoring the activities of competitors: observing their activities in social media, on blogs, in advertisements or cooperation with influencers. • Identification of
  gaps and opportunities: using competitive information to identify areas that can be improved or used as a competitive advantage.

8.9. Effect measurement and optimization

Monitoring the results and optimizing activities are crucial in the process of gaining website traffic. Track the effectiveness of each strategy and make adjustments to achieve better results. To monitor the effects, you can use:

- Website analytics: Tools such as Google Analytics that provide information about website traffic, traffic sources, user behavior and conversions.

- Marketing metrics: indicators such as CTR, CPA, ROI or ROAS that will allow you to assess the effectiveness of marketing activities.

- A/B tests: experiments that will allow you to check which elements (eg titles, content, CTA) are more effective and increase website traffic.

By optimizing your activities, you will be able to use the most effective strategies for gaining traffic on your website, which will allow you to achieve your goals related to the development and conversion of users.

It is also important to analyze the activities of competitors and monitor and optimize your own strategies to achieve better results and consistently develop your business.

Chapter 9: Website Optimization (landing pages)

Landing pages, also known as landing pages, are a key element in the process of acquiring new customers and increasing conversions. In this chapter, you'll learn how to optimize your landing pages to attract more users and encourage them to take a specific action.

9.1. What is a landing page?

A landing page is a website where a user lands after clicking on an advertising link, search result or social media post. Landing pages are designed to focus on one specific goal, such as signing up for a newsletter, purchasing a product, or downloading an e-book.

9.2. Effective landing page elements

- Attractive and legible headline: it should catch the user's attention and quickly convey the value of the offer.

- Short and convincing description: show the benefits related to the offer that will convince the user to take action.

- Visualizations: images, infographics or videos that will attract the user's attention and help understand the offer.
- Contact form or action button (CTA): encouraging the user to take a specific action, such as signing up, purchasing or downloading.

- Simple and clear layout: The page should be easy to understand, with an intuitive layout and minimal distractions.

9.3. A well-thought-out content strategy

Creating persuasive and valuable content on your landing page is crucial to its effectiveness. Remember a few rules:

- Focus on the benefits: present the benefits of the offer that will convince the user to take action.

- Choose the right keywords: use keywords that are relevant to your target group and related to your offer.

- Create engaging and persuasive content: use language that will be understandable to your target group and convince them to take action.

9.4. Testing and optimization

Testing different versions of the landing page and elements such as headers, descriptions or CTAs will allow you to optimize its effectiveness. Use A/B tests to compare the results of different versions of the website and introduce optimal solutions.

9.5. Results analysis and monitoring

Monitoring landing page performance and analyzing data will allow you to better understand user behavior and identify areas for improvement. When analyzing the results, pay attention to the following:

- Number of visits: the number of users who have visited the page target.

- Traffic Sources: Channels where users come from (eg ads, social media, search engines).

- Time spent on the site: average time spent by users they spend on the site.

- Bounce Rate: Percentage of visitors who left the page without taking any action.

- Conversion rate: the percentage of users who took the expected action (e.g. subscribed to the newsletter, made a purchase).

Thanks to this, you will be able to evaluate the effectiveness of your landing page and make adjustments to optimize its results.

9.6. Adapting the website to mobile devices

In today's world, more and more users are using mobile devices to browse the internet. Therefore, it is important that your landing pages are responsive and display well on different devices. When optimizing the page under in terms of mobile devices, be sure to pay attention to a few important things:

- Text readability: make sure text is readable on smaller screens and use appropriate font sizes.

- Convenient navigation: make it easy for users scrolling the page, using the menu and touch buttons.

- Loading speed: optimize the size of image files and page code to ensure fast loading on mobile devices.

- Cross-browser compatibility: check that the site displays well on popular mobile browsers.

Optimizing your landing pages is key to attracting more visitors and increasing conversions. Creating attractive, persuasive and valuable content as well as testing and optimizing various elements of the page will allow you to achieve better results.
Also remember to adapt your website to mobile devices to ensure a great user experience, regardless of the device on which they view your website.

9.7. Use of landing page optimization tools

There are many tools that can help you in the landing page optimization process, I especially recommend a few of them:

- Unbounce: Landing page builder and optimization platform with A/B testing features.

- Instapage: a landing page builder and management tool that also offers A/B testing and analytics.

- Google Optimize: A free A/B testing and landing page optimization tool integrated with Google Analytics.

- Hotjar: a tool for analyzing user behavior on website, offering heat maps, session recordings and surveys.

- PageSpeed Insights: a tool from Google to analyze page loading speed and receive optimization recommendations.

9.8. Cooperation with other departments

Landing page optimization is a process that requires collaboration between different departments in an organization, such as marketing, sales, design, and IT. By collaborating with other teams, you can get a fuller picture of user needs, technical capabilities and business goals, which will allow for a better adjustment of the landing page to the requirements and expectations.

As you can see, optimization of landing pages is a key element in the process of acquiring new customers and increasing conversions. Remember to create attractive, convincing and valuable content, test and optimize various elements of the page, adapt it to mobile devices and monitor the results. Use the available tools and collaborate with other departments to create effective landing pages and achieve success in your business.

Chapter 10: Lead Generation Techniques

Lead generation is a key process in the strategy of acquiring new customers. In this chapter, you will learn about various lead generation techniques that will help you grow your lead base and accelerate the growth of your business.

10.1. content mark=ng

Creating valuable and engaging content is one of the effective ways to generate leads. Introducing registration forms, offering free e-books, reports or webinars can encourage users to leave their contact details in exchange for access to valuable materials.

10.2. social media mark=ng

Social media offers a wide range of lead generation opportunities. You can run advertising campaigns, organize contests or publish engaging posts that will attract the attention of users and encourage them to leave their contact details.

10.3. online advertising

Advertising on the Internet, such as Google Ads or Facebook Ads, allows for effective targeting and reaching a wide target group. Well-planned advertising campaigns can generate high-quality leads that are more likely to convert to customers.

10.4. Marke=ng e-mail

Email marketing is a proven way to generate leads. Regularly sending newsletters or special offers can keep recipients interested and encourage them to continue using your offer. Be sure to use segmentation and personalization techniques to reach the right audience and increase the effectiveness of your email campaigns.

10.5. Cooperation with influencers

Cooperation with influencers is a strategy based on using the authority and reach of people who influence their followers. Leveraging influencer recommendations can help build trust in your brand and increase leads.

10.6. Mark=ng viral

Creating content that has the potential to spread quickly across the web can help generate leads. Viral campaigns, funny memes or touching stories can be easily shared by users, which increases the reach of your offer and allows you to reach more potential customers.

10.7. Affiliate networks and affiliate programs

Collaborating with partners such as bloggers, industry experts, and companies with complementary services can help generate leads. Affiliate programs in which participants receive a commission for recommending your offer can be effective in attracting new customers and increasing the reach of your business.

10.8. Website optimization for SEO

High positions in search results are crucial for generating leads. That is why it is important to optimize your website for SEO (Search Engine Optimization), using the right keywords, creating valuable content and taking care of page loading speed and link structure.

10.9. Networking and participation in industry events

Participation in conferences, fairs or other industry events can be a great opportunity to acquire leads.
Networking allows you to establish relationships with potential customers, partners or other specialists in the industry, which can lead to new business opportunities and an increase in the number of leads.

10.10. Webinars and online training

Organizing webinars and online training can be an effective way to generate leads. Webinars allow you to providing valuable information, showing your expertise and establishing relationships with participants who may become potential customers. Be sure to collect attendees' contact information before or after the event so you can continue communicating with them.

We've covered various lead generation techniques that can help you grow your lead base and accelerate your business growth. Remember that the key to success is choosing the right strategy, tailored to your industry, target group and business goals. Regardless of the tactic you choose, remember to monitor and analyze your results and optimize your actions to achieve the best results.

Chapter 11: Viral MarkeUng and how to use it

Viral marketing is a strategy that aims to create content that is easily shared by users, so that the reach of your offer spreads quickly. In this chapter, you'll learn how to put viral marketing into practice and get to know some inspiring examples of using this technique.

11.1. What is mark=ng viral?

Viral marketing is an approach to promotion that involves creating content that has the potential to spread quickly online, primarily through user sharing. The goal of viral marketing is to achieve the greatest possible reach at a relatively low cost, which translates into increasing brand awareness, generating leads and increasing sales.

11.2. How to use marke=ng viral in practice?

1. Create valuable and engaging content: Try to create content that is interesting, exciting, funny, moving, controversial or inspiring.
   It is important that the content matches the needs and interests of your target group.

2. Use Shareable Formats: Viral marketing often relies on easy-to-share formats such as memes, GIFs, short videos, infographics, and articles with interesting photos.

3. Build a community around the brand: Encourage your own followers to actively participate, comment and share content. The larger the community involved, the greater the chance of a viral effect.

4. Monitor trends and current phenomena: Use current events, trends or topics of discussion to create content that can attract users' attention.

5. Work with Influencers: Collaborating with people with high reach and authority in your community can help you achieve greater reach and increase the likelihood of your content being shared.

11.3. Examples of using viral mark=ng

1. Ice Bucket Challenge: In 2014, the campaign of dousing yourself with cold water and nominating more people for this challenge went viral.
The campaign aimed to raise awareness about multiple sclerosis (ALS) and raise funds for research. It gained immense popularity, and numerous celebrities, athletes and people known from social media took part in it.
The Ice Bucket Challenge has raised millions of dollars for research and has become a great example of effective viral marketing.

2. Blendtec: Will It Blend? – Blendtec is a manufacturer of high-end blenders that has created a series of videos called "Will It Blend?". Each episode showcased how their blender handles a variety of unusual items,

such as mobile phones or a golf club. The campaign gained great popularity online, increasing sales of Blendtec products.

3. Old Spice: In 2010, Old Spice created a campaign called "The Man Your Man Could Smell Like", based on a funny and charismatic character who promoted the brand's deodorant. The advertisement quickly gained popularity on the web, and the brand gained a huge number of new customers.

4. Dove: Real Beauty Sketches - In 2013, the Dove brand created a campaign to promote the natural beauty of women and counteract low self-esteem. The campaign was based on a series of videos in which the artist drew portraits of women based on their own descriptions and descriptions of others. The results were compared, showing that women often judge themselves more harshly than others. The campaign has received wide acclaim and has been shared by millions of people around the world.

Viral marketing is an effective strategy that allows you to achieve a large reach and generate leads at a relatively low cost. The key to success is creating valuable and engaging content that will be willingly shared by users. It is also worth observing trends, working with influencers and using different content formats to increase the chances of a viral effect.
Inspirational examples of viral marketing, such as the Ice Bucket Challenge, Blendtec and Dove, show that z

with the right approach, you can achieve spectacular results and increase brand awareness on a large scale.

Chapter 12: Using Social Media to Acquire Customers

Social media is an integral part of the marketing strategy for many companies that want to acquire new customers and maintain relationships with existing ones. In this chapter, you will learn how to effectively use social media to attract customers.

12.1. The importance of social media

Social media, such as Facebook, Instagram, Twitter, LinkedIn or TikTok, allow you to build a community around your brand, interact with customers and promote your products and services. They are also an excellent source of information about the needs and preferences of customers, which can help in better adapting the offer to market expectations.

12.2. Social media strategy

The key to success in using social media is to develop a coherent and well-thought-out strategy. The following items should be considered:

1. Goals: Define what you want to achieve with your social media presence - is it boosting

brand awareness, acquiring new customers, building loyalty or sales support.

2. Target audience: Specify who you are targeting activities in order to be able to adapt the content and communication to the needs and interests of its recipients.

3. Choosing platforms: Consider which social media is most relevant to your brand and target audience. Each of the platforms has its own unique features and capabilities that are worth taking advantage of.

4. Content planning: Develop a publishing calendar that will help you publish engaging content on a regular basis, tailored to your chosen platforms and target audience.

12.3. Techniques of customer acquisition in social media

1. Create engaging content: Publish valuable, interesting and engaging content that will be eagerly commented and shared by users.

2. Interaction with users: Be active in communicating with your followers, respond to comments, questions and messages to build customer relationships.

3. Organization of contests and promotions: Contests, giveaways or promotions are a great way to increase your reach and gain new followers and

potential customers.

4. Collaboration with influencers: Collaboration with individuals with a large reach and authority in their community can help you achieve greater reach and increase the likelihood of acquiring new customers.

5. Paid advertising: Use paid post promotions to reach a wider audience and precisely target your campaigns.

6. Performance Monitoring: Track metrics such as follower count, engagement, conversions, and website traffic to evaluate your performance and make adjustments if necessary.

7. Using storytelling: Tell stories related to your brand, products or customers to build emotional connections with your audience and increase their engagement.

12.4. Examples of effective use of social media in customer acquisition

1. Airbnb: This company uses Instagram to post beautiful photos of the interiors offered by its hosts. Users often tag their photos with the hashtag #airbnb, which increases reach and attracts new customers.

2. Starbucks: Starbucks is active on many social media platforms where it publishes a variety of content, such as information about new products, inspiring photos and trivia. This company is also famous for organizing competitions that increase the reach and engagement of recipients.

3. Tesla: This brand often uses Twitter to publish news, achievements and entries related to the future of the automotive industry. Tesla CEO Elon Musk actively uses his profile to communicate with users and engage them in discussions.

Social media plays a key role in attracting new customers and maintaining relationships with existing ones. By using the right strategy, engaging content and techniques such as competitions, cooperation with influencers or paid advertising, you can effectively increase your reach, acquire new leads and support sales. Remember that the key to success is to adapt your strategy to the needs and interests of the target group and selected social media platforms.

Part III: Retention and development of existing customers

In previous chapters, we discussed strategies for acquiring new customers through growth hacking techniques and the use of social media. In this section of the book, we will focus on maintaining and developing relationships with existing customers, which is equally important to the long-term success of your business. Understanding the needs and expectations of your current customers and fostering their loyalty can bring significant benefits to your brand, such as increasing Customer Lifetime Value or gaining new customers through recommendations.

Chapter 13: Retention and Development of Existing Customers

Customer retention is crucial for any business. Long-term customer relationships allow for increased customer lifetime value, which in turn leads to higher revenues and profits. In addition, acquiring new customers is often more costly than retaining existing ones, so maintaining customer loyalty is essential to a company's profitability. Loyal customers are also more likely to recommend your brand to others, which can help you attract new customers.

13.2. Understanding customer needs and expectations

The key to customer retention is understanding their needs and expectations and delivering value that exceeds their expectations. Various methods can be used to do this, such as:

1. Market Research: Do regular research to get to know the opinions of customers about your brand, products or services.

2. Analytics: Use analytics tools to track customer behavior on the website, shopping preferences, and promotion effectiveness.

3. Communication with customers: Encourage customers to share their opinions, needs or problems through various communication channels, such as social media, e-mail and telephone support.

13.3. Customer retention strategies

Here are some strategies to help you keep and grow your existing customers:

1. Excellent customer service: Provide prompt and competent customer service that will help solve problems, answer questions and build positive relationships.

2. Personalization: Deliver personalized offers, content or recommendations that reflect the needs and interests of customers. Leverage the data collected during your interactions with customers to better understand their preferences and adjust your actions.

3. Loyalty Programs: Enter programs loyalty programs that reward customers for frequent purchases, recommendations or other activities. These programs may include points, discounts, exclusive promotions or gifts.

4. Communication and engagement: Inform regularly customers about news, special offers or important events related to your brand. Create engaging content that will engage customers and

keep them up to date.

5. Improving products and services: Continuously work on improving your offer, taking into account the needs and expectations of customers. Bug reports, suggestions or customer feedback can be a valuable source of information for improvement.

6. Customer Satisfaction Monitoring: Measure customer satisfaction through surveys, surveys, and review analysis to assess your brand satisfaction and identify areas for improvement.

13.4. Examples of companies that successfully retain and develop customers

1. Amazon: This company is famous for its excellent customer service and fast execution of orders. Amazon Prime is a loyalty program that offers customers access to free delivery, exclusive promotions and video content.

2. Apple: The Apple brand builds customer loyalty by offering innovative products, excellent customer service and maintaining a consistent and attractive brand image.

3. Zappos: Specializing in shoes and apparel, Zappos has won over customers with exceptional customer service, free shipping and a simple return process.

Retaining and developing existing customers is crucial to the long-term success of your business. Delivering value that exceeds customer expectations, understanding their needs and using effective customer retention strategies can lead to increased customer lifetime value, loyalty and referrals. By taking care of your current customers, you not only increase the profitability of your company, but also build a strong and lasting brand.

Chapter 14: Customer Engagement Techniques

Customer engagement is a key factor in maintaining and growing your customer base. High engagement means that customers are more interested in your brand, products or services, which translates into greater loyalty, a greater chance for recommendations and an increase in customer lifetime value.
In this chapter, we will introduce you to various customer engagement techniques that you can apply to your growth hacking strategy.

14.1. Gamification

Gamification is the use of game elements such as points, levels or achievements to increase user engagement in various aspects of the activity.
Gamification can take many forms, for example:

1. Loyalty programs with points: Customers earn points for certain actions, such as purchases, recommendations or interactions with the brand. These points can then be exchanged for prizes, discounts or other benefits.

2. Challenges and competitions: Encourage customers to participate in challenges or competitions related to your brand, offering attractive prizes for winners.

3. Achievements and Badges: Give customers badges or achievements for specific actions to motivate them to continue engaging and interacting with the brand.

14.2. Personalization

Personalization is the adaptation of content, offers or communication to the individual needs and preferences of customers. Personalization can take many forms, e.g.:

1. Personalized product recommendations: By analyzing purchase data, you can present customers with products that are most attractive to them.

2. Personalized emails: Send emails containing information about promotions or

news tailored to the interests of customers.

3. Personalization of the website: Adjust the appearance or content of the website to the preferences of customers, e.g. by displaying personalized offers or articles based on their browsing history.

14.3. Community support

Building a strong brand community can significantly increase customer engagement. This can be achieved by:

1. Groups on social media: Create groups on platforms such as Facebook where customers can share their experiences, ask questions or exchange opinions.

2. Online forum: Create an online forum where customers can discuss your brand, products or services, and get support from other users and your team.

3. Brand ambassadors: Encourage your brand enthusiasts to become ambassadors who will promote your products or services on their social networks or blogs.

15.4. Interactive content

Create interactive content that engages customers and forces them to interact with your brand. Examples of interactive content include:

1. Quizzes and Polls: Create quizzes or polls that allow customers to test their knowledge of your brand, products or industry.

2. Webinars and Workshops: Organize online webinars or workshops that help customers gain new knowledge or skills related to your brand.

3. Video tutorials and demos: Create videos that show how to use your products or services and offer practical tips and tricks.

14.5. Email mark=ng

Email marketing is a powerful tool for increasing customer engagement. Here are some tips on how to use email marketing to increase engagement:

1. Mailing List Segmentation: Segment your mailing list based on various criteria such as purchase history, interests or engagement level to send personalized emails.

2. Email Marketing Automation: Leverage marketing automation tools to send personalized emails at the right time, e.g. welcome messages, email reminders

abandoned carts or messages regarding special offers.

3. A/B testing: Perform A/B testing of various
   aspects of your email marketing campaigns, such as email
   subject lines, content, and calls to action, to optimize customer
   engagement.

Increasing customer engagement is essential to retaining and
growing existing customers. The introduction of gamification,
personalization, community support, interactive content or e-mail marketing
can significantly affect customer engagement and translate into
long-term relationships and loyalty. By working to increase customer
engagement, you'll build a stronger brand and secure greater
customer lifetime value.

Chapter 15: Upselling, Cross-selling and Referral Marking

The increase in the company's revenues often depends not only on
acquiring new customers, but also on using the potential of existing ones.
In this chapter, we'll discuss three strategies that help increase
customer value: upselling, cross-selling, and referral markeEng.

15.1. Upselling

Upselling is a technique that encourages a customer to buy a more
expensive product or service instead of the one currently being considered. Here

a few tips on how to effectively implement upselling in your strategy:

1. Understand the customer's needs: Get to know the customer's needs and preferences well so that you can offer him a higher level of product or service that better meets his expectations.

2. Added value: Highlight the benefits of choosing a more expensive option, such as better functionality, a longer warranty, or additional services.

3. Facilitate comparison: Present different variants of products or services side by side, allowing the customer to easily compare and choose the best solution.

4. Incentives: Offer special promotions, discounts or bonuses on choosing a more expensive option to increase the attractiveness of upselling.

15.2. Cross-selling

Cross-selling is a technique that consists in offering the customer additional products or services that complement his current purchase. Here are some tips on how to effectively introduce cross-selling into your strategy:

1. Match the right products: Analyze customer purchases to identify products or services that are often bought together and offer them to customers at the right time.

2. Showcase Added Value: Show how additional products or services can add value and utility to a customer's primary purchase.
3. Personalize your offer: Use customer data, such as their purchase history and preferences, to offer them products and services that are most attractive to them.
4. Take advantage of cross-selling moments: Enable cross-selling at various stages of the purchase path, such as the product page, shopping cart or after-sales email.

15.3. Referral mark=ng

Referral markeEng is about using satisfied customers as brand ambassadors who recommend your products or services to their friends, family or colleagues. Here are some tips on how to successfully introduce referral markEng into your strategy:

1. Encourage referrals: Recommend to satisfied customers attractive referral programs, such as discounts, rewards or rewards for successful referrals.
2. Make it easy to share: Give your customers easy tools to share your offer, such as links, discount codes, and social sharing buttons.

3. Focus on quality: Remember that the best way to winning referrals is to offer quality products and services that satisfy customers.

4. Recognize customer ambassadors: Regularly thank and reward customers who recommend your business. In this way

you maintain their loyalty and engage them for further referrals.

5. Monitor the effectiveness of the referral program: Measure
   the effectiveness of the referral program by analyzing indicators such as
   the number of new customers, the value of referrals or the cost
   of acquiring a customer.

Upselling, cross-selling and referral markeEng are powerful tools to help add value
to your existing customers.
By using these techniques in your strategy, you will not only be able to
increase revenue, but also build long-term relationships with customers,
which translates into greater loyalty and value for your company.

Part IV: Measuring success and optimizing

The last stage of any Growth Hacking strategy consists in assessing the
effectiveness of actions and optimizing them. In this section of the book,
we'll discuss how to measure the effectiveness of different customer acquisition
and retention strategies and how to optimize them for better results.

Chapter 16: Measuring success and optimizing

In the world of Growth Hacking, it is crucial to measure the effectiveness of actions and react quickly to the results obtained. In this chapter, we will discuss what indicators (KPIs) are worth tracking, how to analyze the results, and how to optimize your activities based on these analyses.

16.1. Selection of key indicators (KPIs)

KPIs are key performance indicators that allow you to assess whether your actions are bringing the expected results. Choose the ones that are most relevant to your business, such as:

1. Customer Acquisition Cost (CAC)
2. Customer lifetime value (LTV)
3. Number of new customers
4. Conversion
5. Customer retention rate 6. Number of referrals
7. Email response rate

16.2. Analysis of the results

The analysis of the results allows you to assess which activities are effective and which need optimization. Use analytical tools such as Google AnalyEcs, A/B tesEng or sales funnli analysis to obtain information on the effectiveness of your actions.

16.3. Optimization

Based on the analysis of the results, optimize your strategies.
Here are some tips on how to do that:

1. A/B testing: Run A/B testing to compare
   the effectiveness of different variants of branding elements, such as
   landing pages, emails or ads.

2. Customizing your strategies: Based on your results, modify your
   strategies to make them more effective and tailored to your
   customers' needs.

3. Competitive Monitoring: Observe what your competitors are
   doing and learn from their mistakes and successes.

4. Responsiveness: React to the analysis results as soon as possible to
   shorten the time needed to achieve success.

Measuring success and optimizing are key elements of any Growth Hacking
strategy. By choosing the right KPIs, analyzing results and optimizing
activities, you will be able to achieve better results and develop your business
faster.

Chapter 17: KPIs in Growth Hacking - how to measure success

Key performance indicators (KPIs) are an essential element of a growth
hacking strategy. They allow you to measure the effectiveness of actions,

monitor progress and identify areas for optimization. In this chapter, we will discuss the most important KPIs that are worth tracking in growth hacking, how to choose them and how to interpret them.

17.1. Selection of KPIs

Choosing the right KPIs depends on the goals of your company and its specifics. Here are some of the most common metrics to consider
attention:

1. Cost per Customer Acquisition (CAC): The average cost per customer, including spend on branding and sales.

2. Customer lifetime value (LTV): The average amount that a customer brings in over the entire period of cooperation with the company.

3. Conversion rate: Percentage of people who complete the specified action (e.g. purchase, registration) on the website or in the application.

4. Customer Retention: Percentage of customers who stay with the company for a certain period of time.

5. Number of Referrals: Number of new customers acquired through referrals from other customers.
6. E-mail Campaign Effectiveness: Percentage of recipients who they open an email, click on links, or perform other desired actions.

17.2. Interpretation of KPIs

To use KPIs effectively, you need to be able to interpret them. Here are some tips on how to do it:

1. Compare results: Compare results across different activities, channels or time periods to identify what works best.

2. Set Goals: Set goals for each KPI you would like to achieve and monitor your progress towards them.

3. Analyze trends: Observe changes in KPIs on over time to understand how your actions affect your results.

4. Learn from mistakes: If any KPIs are not achieving the expected values, think about what can be improved and what actions can be taken to improve them.

17.3. Optimization based on KPIs

Based on KPIs analysis, optimize your growth hacking strategy. Some optimization techniques include:

1. A/B testing: Perform A/B testing to compare the performance of different variants of your branding elements, such as landing pages, emails, and ads.

2. Prioritize: Focus on those activities that have the greatest impact on your most important KPIs, and redirect resources to optimizing them.

3. Strategy adaptation: Based on KPIs results, adjust its strategy to changing market conditions and customer needs and expectations.

4. Automation: Use tools that automate marketing, sales and analytics processes to save time and resources and better track KPIs.

KPIs in growth hacking are essential tools that allow you to measure the success of marketing and sales activities and optimize them. By choosing the right metrics, interpreting them, and using them to make decisions, you'll gain better control of your growth strategy and be able to achieve your business goals more effectively. Remember that the key to success in growth hacking is constant monitoring of KPIs, testing new ideas and adapting to changing market conditions.

Chapter 18: A/B Testing and Experimentation

Experimentation plays a key role in growth hacking.
By running tests and analyzing the results, we can understand
what actions bring the best results and optimize our strategies. A/B
testing is one of the most popular experimentation methods
that allows you to compare the performance of different variants of
markeng elements, such as landing pages, emails or ads. In this
chapter, you'll learn how to run A/B tests and how to use
experimentation to succeed in growth hacking.

18.1. What are A/B tests?

A/B testing involves comparing two variants of a branding
element, such as a landing page, email, or ad, to determine which
one yields better results. The test involves randomly assigning
users one of the variants (A or B) and then analyzing the results to
see which one leads to a higher conversion rate or other key
performance indicator (KPI).

18.2. How to conduct A/B tests?

1. Define your goal: Before running an A/B test, define your
   experiment goal, such as increasing the conversion rate on
   your landing page or improving the performance of your email campaign.

2. Select an item to test: Decide which item
   you want to test, e.g. headline, image or CTA button (call

to aceon).

3. Create variants: Create two versions of the item that will be compared in the test. Variant A should be the current version, while Variant B should contain the change you want to test.

4. Divide traffic or audience: Utilize the tools to A/B testing to randomly divide website traffic or email recipients into two groups. One group will see Option A and the other will see Option B.

5. Track Results: Track test results such as conversion rates, i compare them between variants A and B.

6. Analyze and draw conclusions: After completing the test, analyze the results and decide which variant is better. Draw conclusions and apply changes to your markeeng strategy.

18.3. Best practices in A/B testing

1. Test one variable at a time: For reliable results, only test one variable at a time. Otherwise, it will be difficult to determine which change affected the result.

2. Set an appropriate test duration: A/B tests should be long enough to get enough data.
Too short a duration may lead to erroneous conclusions.

3. Assure statistical significance: Ensure that the differences between options A and B are statistically significant. You can do this using the statistical significance calculators available online.

4. Carefully analyze the results: Look at the A/B test results to understand why the variant performed better. This will allow you to draw conclusions and generate ideas for further tests.

5. Keep testing: Keep experimenting after one A/B test. Growth hacking is based on continuous testing and optimization. Use the results of previous tests to plan the next ones.

18.4. Experimentation as a philosophy of growth hacking

Experimentation is a key element of the growth hacking philosophy. By constantly testing various ideas, strategies and tactics, growth hackers strive to optimize processes and increase the effectiveness of markEng activities. Here are some tips on how to use experimentation in growth hacking:

1. Establish Hypotheses: Before conducting an experiment, formulate a hypothesis that you want to test. The hypothesis should be based on data and previous observations.

2. Prioritize experiments: Given limited resources, value and prioritize the experiments they have

the greatest potential to influence KPIs.

3. Measure Effectiveness: Use KPIs to measure
effectiveness of experiments and comparison of results.
Monitor progress and draw conclusions.

4. Learn from mistakes: Not every experiment will end
success. It's important to learn from failed attempts and adjust your
strategy based on those lessons.

A/B testing and experimentation are key elements of growth hacking.
They allow you to understand what actions bring the best results and
optimize your markeeng strategies. Be sure to perform A/B testing
according to best practices, such as testing one variable at a time,
ensuring statistical significance, and continuously monitoring the results.
Experimentation should be treated as a philosophy of growth hacking,
based on continuous testing, analysis of results and optimization of
processes.

Incorporating experimentation and A/B testing into your marketing
strategy can bring numerous benefits, such as increasing the conversion
rate, user engagement, as well as improving the profitability of your
marketing campaigns. Above all, however, experimenting allows you
to gain valuable information about your target group, their needs and
preferences, which in turn allows you to develop even more effective
growth strategies for your business.

Chapter 19: Web analytics and its application in Growth Hacking

Web analytics is an inseparable element of growth hacking, allowing you to measure the effectiveness of actions, analyze user behavior and identify areas that require optimization.
In this chapter, we'll discuss what web analytics is, what tools are available, and how to use data analytics to drive growth.

19.1. What is web analytics?

Web analytics is the process of collecting, measuring, analyzing and reporting data about users and their behavior on websites. The purpose of web analytics is to understand how users use the site, what elements bring the best results, and identify areas for improvement.

19.2. Web analytics tools

There are many web analytics tools that can help you analyze data and monitor the effectiveness of your marketing efforts.
Here are some popular tools:

1. Google AnalyEcs - the most popular analytics tool
   website that offers a wide range of functions, such as traffic analysis, user behavior, conversion or integration with other Google tools.

2. Hotjar - a tool for analyzing user behavior that allows you to create heat maps, record user sessions and conduct surveys.

3. Mixpanel – an advanced analytics tool that allows you to track events, analyze data in real time and segment users.

4. Kissmetrics - a tool focused on analysis individual user behavior, conversions and optimization of markEng activities.

19.3. Key web analytics metrics

Web analytics allows you to track many metrics that are important for growth hacking. Here are some of them:

1. Website traffic - number of visits, page views, unique users and time spent on the website.

2. Traffic sources - information on the channels from which the traffic comes, such as search engines, social media or advertising.

3. Conversion rates - an indicator that shows how often users perform specific actions, e.g. make a purchase or sign up for a newsletter.

4. User behavior - analysis of navigation paths, exit pages or interaction with website elements.
5. E-commerce metrics - indicators such as basket value, number of orders or customer lifetime value (LTV).

19.4. The use of web analytics in Growth Hacking

Web analytics is a key element of the process of optimizing and achieving growth in growth hacking. Here are some ways you can use data analytics in your operations:

1. Identification of weak points: Analytics allows you to identifying areas where users encounter problems, such as pages with a high bounce rate or low conversion. Based on this information, you can make corrections and optimize your website.

2. Optimization of traffic channels: Analysis of traffic sources allows you to understand which channels bring the most valuable visitors and conversions. You can then focus on optimizing these channels as well as looking for new traffic sources.

3. Testing and Experimentation: Web analytics allows you to monitor the results of the A/B tests and experiments you run as part of your growth hacking strategy. You can analyze on an ongoing basis

results, make changes, and continue testing.

4. Personalization and segmentation: Thanks to web analytics, you can collect information about your users and group them according to various criteria, such as demographics, behavior or traffic sources. This allows you to personalize communication and create targeted marketing campaigns.

5. Measuring the effectiveness of activities: Web analytics allows you to track key performance indicators (KPIs) and assess the effectiveness of marketing activities. Based on this data, strategies and tactics can be adjusted to achieve better results.

Web analytics is an essential tool in growth hacking that allows you to analyze data, identify areas for optimization and measure the effectiveness of activities. Using web analytics, we can understand how users use our website, what elements bring the best results and what traffic channels are the most valuable. Thanks to this, we can make better decisions, optimize our operations and achieve growth at the scale of the enterprise.

Chapter 20: Process optimization and continuous improvement

In growth hacking, the approach to continuous improvement, process optimization and experimentation is key. By focusing on development and improvement, you can achieve growth and maintain competitiveness on the market. In this chapter, we will discuss how to optimize business processes, how to implement continuous improvement, and how to use this approach in a growth strategy.

20.1. Process optimization

Process optimization consists in analyzing and improving business processes in order to increase their efficiency, reduce costs and improve quality. To optimize processes in your company, you should:

1. Identify Existing Processes: Analyze the processes that occur in the organization, such as sales, markeEng, customer service or production.

2. Understand how processes affect business success: Identify which processes have the greatest impact on achieving business goals and focus on optimizing them.

3. Measure process effectiveness: Establish process performance indicators (KPIs) such as lead times, costs, and quality to assess which ones need improvement.

4. Make improvements and modifications: Develop improvement plans, such as automating tasks, eliminating redundant steps, or changing the order of tasks.

5. Monitor results and make further changes: Track the effects of your improvements, analyze the results and continue optimizing to achieve better results.

20.2. Continuous improvement

Continuous improvement is a philosophy that assumes that there is always room for improvement, even if the process is working well. In order to introduce continuous improvement in your organization, it is worth:

1. Promote a culture of continuous improvement: Encourage employees to look for opportunities for improvement, take initiatives and experiment.

2. Experiment: Test different solutions, approaches or technologies to see if they can bring better results to your processes.

3. Analyze the results: Monitor the results of experiments, tests and improvements to understand which activities are working as expected and which need further modifications.

4. Collaborate and share knowledge: Create a space for collaboration and knowledge sharing between departments and employees to learn from each other and implement improvements faster.

5. Learn from mistakes: Mistakes are inevitable, but it is crucial to treat them as a source of knowledge and experience. Analyze mistakes, draw conclusions and make changes to avoid repeating them.

20.3. Optimization and continuous improvement in Growth Hacking

In the context of growth hacking, process optimization and continuous improvement are extremely important, as they allow for faster achievement of growth goals. To apply these principles to your growth hacking strategy, keep the following in mind:

1. Hypothesis testing: Make hypotheses about what might affect growth, run experiments, and analyze the results to understand what works.

2. Adaptation to changing market conditions:
Optimize your growth strategy based on changing market trends,
competition or customer preferences.

3. Keeping the pace of innovation: Don't rest on your laurels -
always look for new solutions, tools or techniques that can contribute
to the growth of your business.

4. Optimization of the conversion path: Analyze and optimize the path,
that customers go through from the first contact with your brand to
purchase to increase conversion and customer lifetime value (LTV).

5. A broad approach to optimization: Remember that process optimization
does not only apply to marketing activities, but also to other
business areas, such as sales, customer service or logistics.

Process optimization and continuous improvement are key to the success
of growth hacking. By systematically analyzing, testing and modifying
processes, you can achieve better results, increase efficiency and
achieve growth. Remember that continuous improvement is not only a
matter of optimizing marketing activities, but also all other business
aspects. Promote a culture of continuous improvement in your
organization, encourage experimentation and adaptation to changing
market conditions to achieve long-term success.

20.4. Automation and technology in process optimization

The introduction of modern technologies and the automation of certain tasks can contribute to streamlining processes and achieving greater growth. In this context, it is worth noting on:

1. Automation Tools: Utilize tools and software, such as markEng machines, CRM, or content management systems (CMS) to automate tasks that are time-consuming and monotonous.

2. Systems integration: Connect various systems and tools used in the organization so that data can flow freely between them, which will allow for faster decision making and better internal communication.

3. Artificial intelligence and machine learning: Take advantage the potential of artificial intelligence and machine learning to optimize processes, forecast trends and understand customer needs and behavior.

4. Data analytics: Use analytics tools to analyze huge amounts of data obtained from various sources and draw conclusions from them that will allow for optimization of activities.

5. Innovative technologies: Stay up to date with new ones technologies that can impact your business, such as

The Internet of Things, blockchain or cloud-based solutions that can contribute to the optimization of processes.

20.5. A culture of experimentation and continuous learning

Introducing a culture of experimentation and continuous learning in the organization is crucial for maintaining innovation and continuous improvement. In practice, this means:

1. Creating conditions for experimentation: Provide your employees with the space, time and resources that will allow them to conduct experiments, test new ideas and solutions.

2. Acceptance of errors: Treat errors as part of the learning and optimization process. Instead of punishing mistakes, encourage learning and improvement in the future.

3. Share knowledge and experience: Promote openness and exchange of knowledge and experience between employees and departments, which will allow for faster implementation of improvements and better understanding of business needs.

4. Invest in employee development: Provide your employees with the opportunity to participate in training, conferences or workshops that will allow them to acquire new skills and broaden their knowledge.

5. Collaborate: Collaborate with other companies,
   experts or scientific institutions that can provide new perspectives,
   knowledge or technologies that can contribute to the optimization
   of processes in your organization.

Continuous improvement and optimization of processes are essential for success in growth hacking. The introduction of a culture of experimentation and continuous learning will allow for ongoing adaptation of the growth strategy to changing market conditions, as well as faster achievement of business goals. Investing in the development of employees, promoting cooperation and the use of modern technologies will allow us to maintain competitiveness and long-term success on the market.

Part V: Success stories of Growth Hacking

In this section of the book, we look at some great examples of companies that have achieved success using growth hacking strategies.
Understanding how these organizations have applied different growth techniques will allow you to be inspired by their achievements and apply these strategies to your own business.

Chapter 21: Success stories of Growth Hacking

The successes of these companies show that the use of growth hacking strategies can bring significant results. Their achievements prove that regardless of the industry or type of product, an innovative approach to attracting customers, maintaining their loyalty and striving for continuous development can lead to long-term success on the market. Based on these examples, it is worth considering what growth hacking strategies can be used in your own business to also achieve spectacular results.

21.1. Dropbox case studies

Dropbox, a cloud storage company, is one of the best-known examples of growth hacking success. Founded in 2007 by Drew Houston and Arash Ferdowsi, Dropbox has revolutionized the way files are stored and shared online. Let's analyze in detail how the company achieved success thanks to its growth hacking strategy.

Challenge

Dropbox started out in the competitive cloud services market. The challenge was to get as many users as possible and encourage them to use the service permanently. The company decided to use a growth hacking strategy to achieve its goals.

referral markEng

Dropbox introduced a referral program that rewarded both referrers and new users with additional storage space. Each user who invited a friend to use Dropbox received an additional 500 MB of storage space. The new user also received an additional 500 MB after creating an account.

This simple and effective solution has grown the number of Dropbox users from 100,000 to 4 million in just 15 months.
The referral program was so effective that 35% of new users were acquired through this mechanism.

Introduction of functions facilitating the use of the service

Dropbox drew attention to the ease of use of the service, introducing features that made storing and sharing files a simple and intuitive process. Automatic synchronization of files between devices, the ability to share files using links or integration with various applications have made Dropbox an indispensable tool for many users.

Cooperation with other companies

Dropbox has established cooperation with other companies, such as Samsung or Adobe, which allowed to increase the reach of the service and attract new users. As part of these partnerships, Dropbox was pre-installed on some smartphones or integrated with popular applications.

Dropbox's success was due to several key factors: an effective referral program, ease of use of the service, and cooperation with other companies. The company has shown that the use of growth hacking strategies can lead to spectacular results and accelerate the growth of the number of users. Thanks to these activities, Dropbox has become one of the leaders in the cloud services industry, with over 700 million users worldwide.

Implementation of freemium as a business model

Dropbox has also adopted the freemium model as part of its growth hacking strategy. This model made it possible to acquire users who could use the basic version of the service for free. Users could increase their account capacity and access additional features by upgrading to paid plans.
This business model made Dropbox attractive to a wide audience, which contributed to the further growth of the number of users.

Investments in user education

In order to increase user engagement and loyalty, Dropbox has invested in educating its customers. The company offered a range of articles, videos and training to help users get the most out of the service. This strategy allowed to maintain long-term relationships with customers, which in turn led to an increase in the number of paid subscriptions.

Achievement awards

Dropbox introduced an achievement rewards system that motivated users to use the service. Users received additional disk space for performing various tasks, such as installing applications on different devices or inviting friends to use the service. This gamification element made using Dropbox more engaging and rewarding.

Conclusions

Dropbox is an excellent example of the success of growth hacking in practice. Thanks to innovative branding strategies, high-quality services and focus on user needs, the company has managed to achieve impressive growth in the number of customers and become one of the leaders in the industry. It is worth analyzing such cases and drawing conclusions that may help in the development of your own ventures by applying the principles of growth hacking.

21.2. Airbnb case studies

Airbnb, a short-term rental platform, is another great example of the effective use of growth hacking strategies. Founded in 2008 by Brian Chesky, Joe Gebbia and Nathan Blecharczyk, the company revolutionized the accommodation market by offering an alternative to traditional hotels. Let's analyze how Airbnb has achieved success using various growth hacking tactics.

Challenge

Airbnb started operations in a difficult market environment, with strong competition from hotels and other plaqorms offering accommodation. The main goal of the company was to attract both property owners and travelers to increase the offer and demand on the plaqorm. To achieve this goal, the company decided to use a growth hacking strategy.

Using an existing plaqorma - Craigslist

One of Airbnb's key moves was the use of an existing online platform - Craigslist. At the time, Craigslist was a popular classifieds website where people posted rental listings. Airbnb developed a mechanism that allowed property owners to post their listings on both the Airbnb platform and Craigslist, thereby increasing the reach of ads and attracting new users.

Improve the quality of photos

Airbnb has realized that the quality of photos is of great importance for the attractiveness of the accommodation offer. Therefore, the company introduced free professional photo sessions for hosts, which contributed to increasing the trust and credibility of the plaqorm among users. The quality of photos has become one of the most important success factors for Airbnb.

Search optimization

Airbnb has invested in optimizing its search algorithms to show users the most relevant accommodations.

Creating a unique, personalized user experience helped increase customer engagement and motivate them to book.

Building trust and security

Airbnb understood that trust is a key element in building a loyal community of users. As a result, the company has introduced various features such as identity verification, a review system, and insurance for hosts. Thanks to these activities, plaqorma has become more attractive and safe for both hosts and guests.

Promotion and referral programs

Airbnb introduced referral programs that encouraged users to recommend the plaqorma to their friends and family. In return for the referral, both the referrer and the person using the recommendation received discounts on future bookings. Thanks to this solution, Airbnb gained a large number of new users for a relatively small cost, using the "power of word-of-mouth branding".

Integration with social media

Airbnb has successfully integrated its plaqorma with social media such as Facebook and Twiler. Users could easily share their travel experiences and search for accommodation based on friends' recommendations. Thanks ago, Airbnb gained greater reach and engagement among its community.

Focus on local communities

Airbnb has understood that local communities are crucial to the growth of the plaqorma. The company invested in the development of local teams that promoted and supported the hosts and guests. This allowed Airbnb to adapt its strategy to the needs and expectations of various markets, as well as to build strong relationships with local communities.

Conclusions

Airbnb is an excellent example of the success of growth hacking in practice. The company has used innovative strategies, user experience optimization and a focus on building trust to achieve spectacular customer growth and become a global leader in the short-term rental market. The analysis of this case study can provide valuable tips for other entrepreneurs who want to achieve success by applying the principles of growth hacking.

21.3. Uber case studies

Uber, a platform for ordering rides via smartphones, is another excellent example of using growth hacking strategies to achieve global success. Founded in 2009 by Travis Kalanick and Garrel Camp, the company revolutionized the transportation market by offering an alternative to traditional taxis.

Let's analyze how Uber used various growth hacking tactics to achieve meteoric growth.

Challenge

Uber started as a small, local business in San Francisco with the intention of meeting the needs of city residents who struggled with taxi scarcity and long waiting times.
The challenge was to convince both drivers and passengers to use the plaqorma and to build trust in the new business model.

Intuitive mobile application

One of the key elements of Uber's success was its intuitive and easy-to-use mobile app. It allowed passengers to quickly order a ride, and drivers - access to information about potential customers. A simple interface and instant notifications made using the application pleasant and convenient for both parties.

Dynamic pricing solutions

Uber introduced dynamic pricing solutions that allowed it to adjust prices to current demand. In periods of greater demand for services, prices increase, motivating drivers to increase availability. Thanks to this system, Uber is able to better manage demand and supply, which translates into greater efficiency and user satisfaction.

Reference programs

Like Airbnb, Uber successfully introduced referral programs that encouraged users to recommend the plaqorma to their friends. In return for the recommendation, the persons recommending and using the recommendation received discounts for future journeys.
As a result, Uber gained new customers and increased the number of service users.

Flexibility for drivers

Uber has created attractive conditions for drivers, offering them the opportunity to earn on their own terms. Drivers can decide their working time, which attracts many new drivers to the plaqorma. Uber also invests in driver training and support, which translates into greater commitment and loyalty to the company.

Expansion into new markets

Uber successfully expanded into new markets thanks to aggressive markeeng strategies and investments in local teams. The company used local events, promotions and cooperation with local influencers to increase brand recognition and gain trust in new cities. Thanks to an effective development strategy, Uber now operates in over 60 countries and hundreds of cities around the world.

Data analytics and optimization

Uber uses data analytics to optimize its services and better understand user needs. The company analyzes data on traffic, waiting times, as well as driver and passenger ratings to constantly improve the quality of services. This allows Uber to make changes and experiment with new ideas that contribute to further growth.

Conclusions

Uber is another great example of using growth hacking to achieve global success. The company used a variety of strategies, such as an intuitive application, reference programs, flexibility for drivers, and expansion into new markets, which allowed it to revolutionize the transport market around the world. The Uber case study provides valuable tips for entrepreneurs who want to succeed by applying the principles of growth hacking.

21.4. Hotmail case studies

Hotmail, founded by Sabir BhaEa and Jack Smith in 1996, is one of the first free email providers. Despite limited funding, Hotmail has become one of the world's largest email service providers, with millions of users in just a few years. In 1997, just 18 months after its launch, Hotmail was acquired by Microsoft for $400 million. Let's analyze how growth hacking made it so spectacularly successful.

Challenge

There were other companies offering free email services in the market, but Hotmail had to find a way to differentiate itself from the competition. The challenge was to get new users without a big budget for markeEng.

Invite a friend (Viral markeEng)

The main growth hacking tactic that contributed to Hotmail's success was placing a simple message at the end of every message sent by users: "PS: I love you. Get your free e-mail at Hotmail." This seemingly innocent add-on served as an effective markEng tool that encouraged e-mail recipients to set up their own Hotmail account. Each Hotmail user unknowingly promoted the service to their friends, families and colleagues.

Low-cost business model

Hotmail decided to provide e-mail services for free, which attracted the attention of many people who did not want to pay for the use of e-mail. Offering a free service was possible thanks to the use of a low-cost business model based on advertisements displayed to users.

Scalability

Hotmail is designed to scale easily as the number of users grows. Thanks to this, even in times rapid growth, the company was able to provide services at a high level, regardless of the number of users.

Hotmail's success is one of the most famous examples of growth hacking in history. The simple but ingenious strategy of embedding a branding message in every email has contributed to reaching millions of users around the world in a very short time.

21.5. Slack case studies

Slack, founded by Stewart Bulerfield in 2013, is a popular communication and collaboration tool for teams. Thanks to its intuitive interface, integration with other applications and advanced features, Slack has won the hearts of millions of users around the world. The company quickly became one of the most valuable startups in the technology industry. Let's analyze how growth hacking made it so successful.

Use of existing users

Slack understood that satisfied users can be the best brand ambassadors. As part of its growth hacking strategy, the company encouraged its users to recommend Slack to others. In exchange for the recommendation, users received benefits such as additional disk space or company gifts.

Focus on product quality

Instead of spending huge sums on markeEng, Slack focused on creating a unique product that will attract users in itself. Thanks to this, the company was able to reduce advertising expenses, and instead invest in the development and improvement of its tool.

Integration with other applications

Slack gained great popularity due to its easy integration with other tools such as Google Drive, Trello or GitHub. By allowing teams to use these apps directly in Slack, the company increased its value to users, which translated into a faster growth rate.

Taking into account the needs of users

Slack constantly developed its platform, listening to the needs of users and introducing new features. Thanks to this, the company was able to keep its users engaged and attract more people who were looking for an effective tool for communication and cooperation.

Development on the B2B market

Slack focused on the B2B market, offering its services to small, medium and large enterprises. The introduction of paid subscription plans that provided additional features and support allowed the company to generate income from customers who needed a more advanced tool.

The success of Slack shows that growth hacking does not have to rely only on innovative markeeng tactics, but also on the proper focus on product quality and understanding the needs of users.

21.6. Tinder case studies

Tinder, the dating app founded in 2012 by Sean Rada, JusEn Mateen, Jonathan Badeen, Joe Munoz, Dinesh Moorjani and Whitney Wolfe, has revolutionized the way people around the world meet and date. The application quickly became one of the most popular in its category, gaining millions of users. Let's analyze how growth hacking made it so successful.

Targeting the right audience

Tinder understood that young people are the most active group among people using dating apps. Therefore, the company decided to target the group of students by organizing events at universities during which participants were encouraged to download the application. This strategy allowed Tinder to gain loyal users who later recommended the app to their friends.

Simplicity and innovation

Tinder introduced an innovative match system based on a simple swipe lex/right gesture.
Users could rate other people's profiles by choosing whether they were interested in making contact. This simplicity and intuitiveness attracted many users who wanted to try a new, simple way to meet other people.

Facebook integration

The Tinder app required users to log in with a Facebook account. This integration allowed the profile to be automatically filled with photos and basic information. Thanks to this, users could quickly start using the application.
In addition, integration with Facebook increased trust in the application and made Tinder gain new users through referrals from friends.

Introduction of paid features

Tinder introduced paid features such as Tinder Plus and Tinder Gold, which offered users additional options such as undoing the last gesture or highlighting a profile. Thanks to this, the company began to generate income from the application, while maintaining a base of free users.

Exploiting international markets

Tinder expanded into international markets, tailoring the app to local needs and preferences. Thanks to this,

the company gained global popularity and became one of the leaders
in the dating application industry.

Conclusions

Tinder's success comes from a combination of innovative ideas, simplicity
of use, and targeting the right audience. Growth hacking used by Tinder
was based on understanding the needs of young users and introducing
a simple but revolutionary profile rating system. Integration with
Facebook increased trust and made the application gain new users
through recommendations from friends.

The use of markeeng strategies at universities, such as organizing
events and promoting the application among students, allowed Tinder
to build a loyal user base. The rapid introduction of paid features enabled
the company to generate revenue and invest in further product
development.

Tinder shows that innovation, understanding the needs of users and focusing
on the right target group can contribute to achieving spectacular success.
For entrepreneurs and marketers, it is worth paying attention to
these elements to apply them in your own markeeng strategies and gain
loyal users.

21.7. Case study Spotify

Spoefy, founded in 2006 by Daniel Ek and MarEn Lorentzon, is one of the most recognizable streaming services in the world.
Offering a wide selection of music and personalized playlists, SpoEfy has attracted millions of users around the world. Let's analyze how growth hacking made it so successful.

Free and paid version

SpoEfy introduced a freemium model that allowed users to use the free version of the service with limitations (e.g. ads) and to buy a premium subscription that offered additional features, such as no ads or the ability to listen to music offline.
This business model allowed for a broad base of users who could then convert into paid subscribers.

Integration with social media

SpoEfy integrated its plaqorma with social media such as Facebook, which allowed users to quickly create accounts and share their favorite music with friends. Thanks to this, SpoEfy gained new users through recommendations and increased the involvement and loyalty of the current ones.

The use of algorithms and data

SpoEfy invested in algorithm development and data analytics to offer users personalized playlists and recommendations. Through features such as "Discover Weekly" or "Daily

Mix", SpoEfy has gained a reputation as a service that can tailor music to the tastes of each listener, increasing user engagement and satisfaction.

Collaboration with artists and labels

SpoEfy has strengthened its position on the market thanks to cooperation with artists and music labels. The service offered exclusive premieres, playlists created by famous artists, and the opportunity for artists to earn money from plays of their songs. Thanks to this, SpoEfy attracted both listeners and creators, increasing its market value.

Expansion into new markets

SpoEfy systematically expanded its activities to new markets, adapting its offer to local needs and preferences. As it gained new users, the company invested in the development of technology and entered into agreements with local creators to better meet the needs of its customers.

SpoEfy's success stems from several key factors. First, the company used a freemium model that attracted a wide range of users who over time became paid subscribers. Secondly, integration with social media made it easy for the site to spread among friends and increase the number of users. Third, investing in algorithms and data analysis allowed for personalized music recommendations that increased engagement and loyalty. Fourth, collaborating with artists and music labels helped build

market value of SpoEfy and attract even more users.
Finally, expanding into new markets and adapting the offer to local needs has allowed SpoEfy to become a global leader among streaming services.

For marketers and entrepreneurs, it is worth paying attention to these elements that contributed to the success of SpoEfy in order to apply them in their own markEng strategies and gain loyal users and increase the reach of their brand.

21.8. Gmail case studies

Gmail, an email service developed by Google, was launched in 2004 as an exclusive invite-only service. Since then, Gmail has revolutionized the email market with over 1.5 billion users worldwide.

Let's analyze how growth hacking made Gmail so successful.

Invitation-only strategy

When Gmail was launched, Google opted for an "invitation-only" strategy - this meant that in order to set up an account with the service, you had to receive a special invitation from an existing Gmail user. This strategy created a great deal of interest and a sense of uniqueness that propelled Gmail to prominence as an exclusive email service. As a result, the number of users grew because new users could also invite their friends.

Offering more space for messages

Gmail introduced a unique feature - a huge amount of free space for messages (1 GB at launch, currently 15 GB). Compared to competitors such as Yahoo! Mail and Hotmail, which offered much less space, Gmail stood out as an attractive alternative for people who needed more space to store their emails.

Innovative features and user interface

Google has invested in the development of innovative features and a clean user interface. Gmail introduced, among others, grouping messages into conversations, spam filtering, quick e-mail search and automatic labeling of messages. These facilities increased the usability of the service and attracted more and more users.

Integration with other Google services

Gmail was one of the first Google products to be integrated with other company services, such as Google Drive, Google Calendar, and Google Hangouts. Thanks to this integration, users could easily use many Google services, which increased customer engagement and loyalty.

Gmail's success stems from several key strategies. First, the invitation-only strategy generated interest and attracted users. Second, the offer of more storage for messages made Gmail stand out in the market. Third, innovative features and a clean user interface made Gmail more and more attractive to users. Fourth, integration with other Google services increased customer engagement and loyalty.

For marketers and entrepreneurs, it is worth paying attention to these elements that contributed to the success of Gmail in order to apply them in their own markEng strategies and gain loyal users and increase the reach of their brand. Learn from the best and adapt these strategies to your product or service to succeed in the market.

In the case of Gmail, growth hacking was based on unique product features, innovation, integration with other services and exclusivity. This allowed Google to build a strong position in the e-mail market and gain a huge user base.
Think about what characteristics and strategies you can use in your business to achieve similar results.

Chapter 22: Polish companies using innovations in markeUng

Case Study 1: Allegro - personalization and product recommendations

Allegro, Poland's largest e-commerce platform, uses markEng innovations to increase customer engagement and sales. One of the key tools used by Allegro is offer personalization and product recommendations based on users' browsing and purchase history. Thanks to the use of artificial intelligence and analysis of large data sets, Allegro is able to provide users with personalized proposals, which increases the chance of attracting customers' attention and making purchases.

Case Study 2: InPost - using social media and content marke=ngu

InPost, an operator of a parcel locker network, uses an innovative approach to markeeng, using social media and content markeeng to increase brand awareness and gain customers. Business creates engaging content, such as articles, guides or videos, which are then published on their website and social media. Thanks to this approach, InPost gains the trust of users and shows its expertise in the field of logistics.

Case Study 3: Booksy - influencer marke=ngu strategy

Booksy, a booking platform for beauty & wellness services, uses influencer markeEng in Poland to reach new customers and increase its user base. By cooperating with local influencers related to the beauty industry, the company promotes its services among potential customers. Thanks to this, Booksy gains the trust of users and becomes recognizable among the competition.

Case Study 4: Bank Millennium - virtual assistant on the website

Bank Millennium, one of the leading banks in Poland, has introduced an innovative solution in the area of customer service - a virtual assistant on its website. This assistant, based on artificial intelligence, answers customers' questions and helps them use the bank's services. Thanks to this solution, Bank Millennium increases customer satisfaction and shortens the response time to their inquiries.

These four cases show how Polish companies use markEng innovations to gain a competitive advantage on the market.
Personalization, content markeEng, influencer markeEng or virtual assistants are just some of the tools that companies can

use it to better understand the needs of your customers and offer them valuable services. Analyze these strategies and consider how you can adapt them to your business to achieve better results.

Case Study 5: Wawel - interactive advertising campaigns

Wawel, a Polish confectionery manufacturer, uses innovative advertising campaigns to engage consumers and increase its brand recognition. One example is a promotional campaign for smarqony, which allowed users to scan QR codes on candy wrappers to unlock special content and offers. Thanks to such interactive campaigns, Wawel gains more interest in its products and strengthens its position on the market.

Case Study 6: Dr Irena Eris - using AR technology in marke=ngu

Dr Irena Eris, a prestigious Polish brand of cosmetics, has introduced an innovative solution in markEng - augmented reality (AR) technology. The company used a mobile application that allowed the cosmetics to be tested on a virtual face model. Thanks to this, customers could see how they will look with given cosmetics before they decide to buy. The use of AR in markEng allowed the Dr Irena Eris brand to increase customer engagement and sales of its products.

Case Study 7: Tauron - gamification in marke=ngu

Tauron, one of the largest Polish energy suppliers, used gamification in markEng, creating an interactive mobile game for its customers. The game educated users on energy saving and promoted ecological behavior. Thanks to gamification, Tauron gained users' involvement, increased its brand awareness and improved its image as a company that cares about the environment.

Case Study 8: 4F - influencer marke=ng and cooperation with sports players

4F, a Polish brand of sportswear, has been successful on the market by using the influencer markeEng and collaborating with sports players. The company cooperates with Polish athletes who promote the brand on their social media profiles by publishing photos and videos related to 4F products. Thanks to this approach, the brand gains recognition, increases trust among customers and builds a strong position on the sportswear market.

Case Study 9: KFC Polska - viral mark=ng and use of humour

KFC Polska, a chain of fast food restaurants, has been successful in markeeng by using viral strategies and using humor in its advertising campaigns. An example is the "KFC on languages" campaign, which consisted in creating funny videos and memes to promote the brand's products. With an approach based on humor and surprising content, KFC Polska has increased its recognition in social media and gained new customers.

Case Study 10: Zalando Polska - marke=ng data driven

Zalando Polska, part of an international e-commerce platform, has succeeded in using data-driven brandEng. The company analyzes user behavior on its website to provide personalized recommendations, promotional offers and email campaigns. Thanks to this approach, Zalando is able to offer its customers more attractive and tailored products, which contributes to the increase in sales and customer loyalty.

All these cases show how Polish companies use innovative branding strategies to increase their market position, win new customers and meet the needs of their customer base. Through various approaches, such as the use of AR technology, gamification, data-driven markEng or influencer markEng, these companies are proving that innovation in markEng can contribute to achieving significant successes.

Case Study 11: Allegro - ads aimed at emotions

Allegro, the largest Polish e-commerce platform, successfully uses advertising campaigns that move the emotions of recipients. An example is their Christmas advertising campaign, which told a touching story of an elderly man learning English. The ad went viral in Poland and abroad, gaining recognition among both customers and the branding industry. Thanks

Thanks to this approach, Allegro has strengthened its image as a brand that cares about the emotions and needs of its customers.

Case Study 12: InPost - innovative logistics services

InPost, a Polish logistics company, has won the recognition of customers by introducing innovative services, such as Paczkomaty - automatic parcel lockers that allow for quick and convenient collection of parcels. The company also uses internet markEng to reach a wide audience and educate them about its services. Thanks to an approach based on innovation and online branding, InPost is enjoying increasing popularity and a growing share in the logistics market.

Case Study 13: Play - collaboration with celebrities

Play, a Polish mobile network, successfully uses the strategy of cooperation with celebrities in its advertising campaigns. The company engages famous personalities such as actors, singers and athletes who promote the network's services in social media, television or on posters. Thanks to this approach, Play gains greater customer trust, increases its recognition and increases the value of its brand.

Case Study 14: CCC - personalization of the offer and the use of e commerce

CCC, a Polish footwear chain, successfully uses offer personalization and e-commerce in its branding strategy. The company analyzes data about customer behavior on its website and in stores to better understand their needs and provide personalized product recommendations. Thanks to this approach, CCC gains customer loyalty, increases sales and maintains its position on the footwear market.

Case Study 15: Wawel - using history and tradition in marke=ngu

Wawel, a well-known Polish confectionery company, has succeeded in using a brandEng based on history and tradition. By presenting its products as part of the Polish cultural heritage, the company has gained the loyalty of many customers and strengthened its position on the confectionery market. Wawel's advertising campaigns often present regional flavors and traditions, which increases consumer interest in their products.

Case Study 16: Orange - gamification in marke=ngu

Orange, a Polish mobile network, successfully uses gamification in its markeeng campaigns. An example is "Orange Ekstraklasa Manager", a mobile game that allows users to manage an Ekstraklasa football team. The game, in addition to promoting the Orange brand, engages users, offers various prizes for winnings and keeps them interested in the company's services.

Case Study 17: ÿywiec - the use of storytelling

ÿywiec, one of the most famous Polish beer brands, has succeeded in using storytelling in its brandEng. ÿywiec's advertising campaigns often tell stories related to the places where the beer comes from, its traditions and culture. Thanks to this approach, ÿywiec gains an emotional bond with customers, increases its recognition and builds its image as a brand with deep cultural roots.

Case Study 18: Pyszne.pl - marke=ng based on data and optimization

Pyszne.pl, a Polish online food ordering platform, successfully uses data-driven and optimization markEng. The company analyzes data about user behavior on its website to provide personalized recommendations, promotional offers and to improve the food ordering process. Thanks to this approach, Pyszne.pl gains customer loyalty, increases sales and maintains its position on the food service market.

Case Study 19: Empik - marke=ng multi-channel

Empik, one of the largest Polish retail chains offering books, music and other cultural products, has been successful using the multi-channel markeEng. The company promotes its products and services through various communication channels, such as TV advertising, Internet advertising, press advertising, posters and social media. In addition, Empik runs a loyalty program that offers customers discounts, special offers and events. Thanks to this approach,

Empik gains customer loyalty, increases sales and maintains its position on the market.

Case Study 20: Tymbark - cooperation with influencers

Tymbark, a Polish company producing fruit drinks, successfully uses cooperation with influencers in its branding strategy. The company engages popular creators from various platforms, such as YouTube, Instagram or TikTok, who promote Tymbark products in their content. Thanks to this approach, Tymbark gains greater customer trust, increases its recognition and increases the value of its brand.

Case Study 21: Kazar - using social media in promotion

Kazar, a Polish footwear and accessories company, has been successful with an active social media promotion strategy. The brand uses platforms such as Instagram, Facebook and Pinterest to show its products in various styles and promote new collections. Thanks to this approach, Kazar gains customer loyalty, increases its recognition and maintains its position on the fashion market.

All these cases show that Polish companies are open to innovations in markEng and successfully introduce new strategies that help them gain a competitive advantage. Thanks to the use of various markeeng techniques, such as storytelling, gamification, data-driven markeeng or cooperation with influencers, Polish companies are able to better understand the needs of their customers, build strong relationships with them and achieve success on the market.

Case Study 22: Cinkciarz.pl - financial education as a marketing tool

Cinkciarz.pl, a Polish fintech specializing in online currency exchange, successfully uses financial education as a marketing tool. The company creates expert articles, guides, webinars and podcasts on topics related to finance and investments, which it offers to its clients for free. Thanks to this approach, Cinkciarz.pl builds trust, increases its recognition and attracts new customers who are more aware of their financial needs.

Case Study 23: InPost - innovative logistics services

InPost, a Polish logistics operator, is successful thanks to the introduction of innovative services, such as Paczkomaty - automatic kiosks for collecting and sending parcels, available 24/7. Thanks to this solution, InPost gains a competitive advantage on the logistics market, offering customers convenient and flexible services. In addition, the company actively uses social media to promote its services and communicate with customers, which contributes to increasing brand recognition.

Case Study 24: CCC - omnichannel and online-offline merger

CCC, one of the largest Polish footwear chains, successfully applies the omnichannel strategy, combining online and offline sales. Business

offers customers the opportunity to purchase products online with home delivery or collection at a selected stationary outlet.
In addition, CCC runs a loyalty program that combines the benefits of online and offline shopping, offering customers special discounts and promotions. Thanks to this approach, the company maintains customer loyalty and increases its sales.

Case Study 25: Zalando Lounge - offer personalization and promotions temporary

Zalando Lounge, a Polish group shopping platform associated with the popular Zalando website, is successful thanks to the use of offer personalization and organizing temporary promotions. The company analyzes customer preferences based on their purchase history and offers them customized products and special discounts.
Thanks to this approach, Zalando Lounge gains customer loyalty and increases its sales.

Polish companies more and more often use innovative marketing methods to gain a competitive advantage on the market. Using the examples of such companies as Allegro, Booksy, Cinkciarz.pl, InPost, CCC or Zalando Lounge, it can be seen that the key to success is flexibility, creativity and the ability to adapt to customer needs.

All these cases show that an innovative approach to markEng, such as the use of growth hacking strategies, offer personalization, omnichannel, the use of new technologies or temporary promotions, allows companies to gain new customers,

increasing sales and maintaining the loyalty of existing customers.
Polish companies have a lot to offer in the field of branding
innovations, and their experience can be an inspiration for other
entrepreneurs looking for new solutions that will allow them to succeed on
the market.

Case Study 26: Bank Millennium - interactive mobile application

Bank Millennium, one of the leading banks in Poland, wins customers
thanks to an innovative and functional mobile application.
The application offers an intuitive interface, personalization and access
to many banking and financial services. The Bank actively promotes
the use of the application by offering special promotions and bonuses
for customers using the application. Thanks to this approach, Bank
Millennium gains a competitive advantage on the market and
increases customer involvement.

Case Study 27: Pyszne.pl - making online orders easier

Pyszne.pl, a popular Polish online food ordering platform, is successful
thanks to its innovative approach to customer service.
The company allows customers to quickly and conveniently order food
from local restaurants, and offers a variety of payment methods, including
online and cash on delivery. Pyszne.pl regularly offers promotions
and discounts that attract new customers and keep existing ones
loyal. The introduction of the mobile application made it easier to
order food on the phone, which increased traffic and sales.

Case Study 28: Play - advertising campaigns and loyalty
programs

Play, one of the leading Polish mobile telephony networks, is
successful thanks to creative advertising campaigns and attractive
loyalty programs. The company gains customers through
humorous and original advertisements that draw attention and build
a positive brand image. In addition, Play offers the Play Club
loyalty program, which allows customers to collect points for using
network services and exchange them for prizes. Thanks to this
approach, Play maintains customer loyalty and attracts new
users.

Case Study 29: eobuwie.pl - product recommendations and virtual
fitting room

eobuwie.pl, a Polish online footwear and accessories store, is
successful thanks to innovative features such as product
recommendations and a virtual fitting room. The store analyzes
customer preferences based on their purchase history
and offers them personalized product recommendations. The virtual
fitting room allows customers to try on selected footwear virtually,
which reduces the number of returns and increases customer
satisfaction. Thanks to this approach, eobuwie.pl gains customer
loyalty and gains new users, which translates into an increase in sales.

Case Study 30: Empik - omnichannel solutions and offer development

Empik, a Polish chain of bookstores and shops with a diverse cultural offer, is successful thanks to its omnichannel strategy and continuous development of its offer. Empik introduces new technologies, such as a mobile application or virtual gift cards, which make it easier for customers to shop and access the offer. The company also offers a wide selection of courses, trainings and workshops that enrich the offer and attract different groups of customers. Thanks to this approach, Empik gains a competitive advantage on the
market and maintains customer loyalty.

Case Study 31: iTaxi - easy taxi ordering and competitive prices

iTaxi, the Polish application for ordering taxis, wins customers thanks to the ease of use of services and competitive prices. The company allows customers to quickly and conveniently order a taxi using an application that tracks the user's location and allows the selection of the nearest available taxi driver. iTaxi often offers promotions and discounts that attract new customers and maintain the loyalty of existing ones. Thanks to this approach, iTaxi gains an advantage on the urban transport market.

Examples of companies in Poland that are successful thanks to innovations in markEng show that the key to success is flexibility, creativity and the ability to adapt to customer needs.
Regardless of the industry, companies must take risks and experiment with new solutions to gain a competitive advantage in the market. An innovative approach to markEng, as the examples show, translates into gaining new customers, increasing sales and maintaining the loyalty of existing customers.

Case Study 32: Allegro - innovative mark=ng strategies and plasorma development

Allegro, the largest Polish e-commerce platform, is successful thanks to innovative markEng strategies and continuous development of its platform. The company invests in online and offline advertising, often creating humorous campaigns that capture the attention of the audience.
In addition, Allegro is constantly introducing new features and services, such as Allegro Smart! or Allegro Lokalnie to facilitate shopping for customers and meet their needs. Thanks to these initiatives, Allegro maintains its leading position on the e-commerce market in Poland.

Case Study 33: InPost - fast and convenient parcel delivery

InPost, a Polish logistics operator, wins customers thanks to innovative solutions in the area of parcel delivery. The company offers delivery services using Parcel Lockers, which enable customers to collect parcels at any time, without having to wait for the courier. InPost also introduces additional services, such as the possibility of returning goods through Paczkomaty, which makes it easier for customers to use the company's services. By investing in the development of the Paczkomaty network and applying an innovative approach to branding, InPost gains a competitive advantage on the logistics market.

Case Study 34: GetResponse- marke=ng automa=on and services for entrepreneurs

GetResponse, a Polish company offering online branding tools, wins customers thanks to innovative services for entrepreneurs. The company offers tools for markeeng automaEon, e-mail markeeng and conducting webinars that facilitate communication with customers and obtaining leads. GetResponse also introduces new features and integrations with popular e-commerce platforms, which allows for faster and more effective marketing activities. By investing in the development of its services and offering valuable tools for entrepreneurs, GetResponse gains a competitive advantage on the market of markEng tools.

Examples of Polish companies that are successful thanks to innovative solutions in markEng show that the key to success is continuous improvement of the offer, flexibility and the ability to adapt to the changing needs of customers. Innovations in markEng contribute to gaining a competitive advantage on the market, which translates into an increase in sales.

Case Study 35: Booksy - booking services online

Booksy is a Polish company that offers a plaqorma for booking online services, such as hairdressing, cosmetics or fitness. Thanks to an innovative approach to booking, the company gains the trust of customers who can easily and quickly book their appointments. Booksy uses internet markEng and social media to reach its target group by creating valuable content and engaging campaigns.

Case Study 36: Ithaca - dream travels with the use of technology

Itaka, a leading Polish tour operator, uses markEng innovations to provide its customers with unforgettable holidays. The company uses advanced technologies, such as virtual reality or chatbots, to make it easier for customers to choose an offer and communicate with the company. Itaka also runs effective markEng campaigns in social media and on
video plaqorms that attract the attention of recipients.

Case Study 37: MyBzz - establishing business relations

MyBzz is a mobile application for establishing business relationships quickly, easily and effectively. It allows you to gain contacts necessary for the development of your company economically and ecologically, because the only thing you need to use this tool is your smartphone and Internet access. The app has functionalities that are extremely useful for every entrepreneur. It helps to change contacts into contracts, but also to open one's head to something new. You can download the app for free from the App Store or Google Play - see you on MyBzz

Case Study 38: Whisbear - innovative toys for children

Whisbear is a Polish company that designs and produces innovative toys for children, such as mascots with white noise function. The company uses original ideas and advanced technology to make create products that support the development of children and help them in everyday functioning. Whisbear also runs effective marketing campaigns in social media that increase brand awareness and attract new customers.

Case Study 39: Rebel.pl - board games for everyone

Rebel.pl is a Polish company that distributes board and card games. Thanks to its innovative approach to markEng, the company is gaining popularity among game lovers, offering attractive promotions, contests and engaging content in social media.

Case Study 40: Brand24 - social media monitoring

Brand24 is a Polish company offering a social media monitoring and online brand management tool. Thanks to an innovative approach to data analysis and advanced algorithms, Brand24 helps entrepreneurs in monitoring and analyzing their presence in social media and brand perception by customers. The company uses various markeEng strategies, such as content markeEng or influencer markeeEng, to increase its popularity and acquire new customers.

Case Study 41: LiveChat - real-time customer support

LiveChat is a Polish company that offers a real-time customer service tool via chat on the website. Thanks to an innovative approach to communication with customers, LiveChat helps entrepreneurs in building customer relationships, increasing customer engagement and satisfaction. The company uses a variety of markeeng strategies, such as content markeeng, e-mail campaigns or cooperation with influencers to gain new customers.

Case Study 42: Duka - expansion into foreign markets

Duka is a Polish company offering products for the kitchen and dining room, which has been successful thanks to innovative branding strategies and expansion into foreign markets. The company runs effective markeeng campaigns, such as seasonal promotions, competitions and cooperation with influencers, to increase its popularity in Poland and abroad. Duka constantly introduces new products to its offer to meet customer expectations and gain a competitive advantage on the market.

Case Study 43: Inelo - innovative solutions for the transport industry

Inelo is a Polish company that offers innovative solutions for the transport industry, such as driver working time control systems or tachograph data analysis. Thanks to advanced technology and innovative ideas, Inelo wins the trust of customers who want to improve the efficiency and safety of their fleet of vehicles. The company uses various markeeng strategies, such as content markeeng, industry conferences or social media campaigns, to gain new customers and strengthen its position in the market.

Case Study 44: Zortrax - 3D printing at a high level

Zortrax is a Polish company specializing in the production of 3D printers and printing materials. Thanks to innovative technological solutions, Zortrax gains the trust of customers around the world who are looking for high-quality 3D printing devices. The company uses various markeeng strategies, such as content markeeng, participation in trade fairs or engaging social media campaigns to gain new customers and increase its popularity.

Case Study 45: MakoLab - digital services for enterprises

MakoLab is a Polish company that offers digital services for enterprises, such as creating websites, mobile applications, software and online branding. Thanks to an innovative approach to technology and a wide range of services, MakoLab gains the trust of customers who want to strengthen their online presence and gain a competitive advantage on the market. The company uses various markeeng strategies, such as content markeeng, organizing webinars or cooperation with business partners to gain new customers and develop its services.

Case Study 46: G2A - video game plasorma

G2A is a Polish online plaqorma that offers video games, game keys and other gaming-related products. Thanks to innovative technological solutions, attractive prices and a wide range of products offered, G2A wins the trust of players around the world. The company uses a variety of branding strategies, such as sponsoring esports teams, engaging social media campaigns, and collaborating with influencers to gain new customers and increase its popularity.

Case Study 47: X-Trade Brokers - online investment services

X-Trade Brokers (XTB) is a Polish company offering online investment services, such as trading on the Forex market, CFDs and binary options. Thanks to innovative technological solutions, such as advanced transactional platforms and analytical tools, XTB gains the trust of clients who want to invest in financial markets. The company uses various markeeng strategies, such as content markeeng, participation in industry conferences or engaging campaigns in social media.

Case Study 48: Symplur - technologies for healthcare

Symplur is a Polish company that offers innovative technologies for the healthcare sector, such as plaqorms for patient data management or medical data analysis. Thanks to advanced technological solutions, Symplur gains the trust of customers who want to improve the quality of healthcare and improve the management of medical facilities. The company uses various markEng strategies, such as content markEng, participation in industry conferences or engaging campaigns in the media social networks to gain new customers and strengthen your position in the market.

Case Study 49: Veriori - jewelry with technology

Veriori is a Polish company that designs and produces innovative jewelry with built-in technology, such as smart rings or bracelets. Thanks to unique solutions that combine the elegance of jewelry with practical functions, such as activity monitoring or message notifications, Veriori wins the trust of customers who are looking for fashionable and functional accessories. The company uses various markeeng strategies, such as content markeeng, cooperation with influencers or engaging social media campaigns to gain new customers and increase its popularity.

Case Study 50: Linkbot.pl - automation of mark=ngu, sales and customer service

Linkbot is a tool that helps automate sales, markeng and employee acquisition processes in the company. This tool is based on artificial intelligence and machine learning technologies that help in data analysis, identifying trends and making decisions.

In sales, Linkbot helps automate the lead generation process by sending personalized emails or direct messages on plaqorms social. Linkbot can also automatically remind you of important sales deadlines and tasks.

In markEng, Linkbot helps automate the process of managing advertising campaigns and communicating with clients. This tool can help in analyzing data on customer preferences and adjusting marketing communication to their needs.

In acquiring employees, Linkbot helps in automating the process of searching and screening candidates for positions in the company. This tool can help you analyze data from job profiles and other sources, such as employee databases, and send you personalized emails with job offers.

Linkbot helps in saving time and increasing the efficiency of business processes, which can contribute to improving the company's financial results.

The analysis of cases of Polish companies that are successful thanks to innovative solutions in markEng shows that the key to success is continuous improvement of the offer, flexibility and the ability to adapt to the changing needs of customers. Innovations in markEng contribute to gaining a competitive advantage on the market, which translates into an increase in sales and maintaining the leading position in the industry. Polish companies that are able to use innovations in markEng have a chance for dynamic development and gaining the trust of customers around the world.

End

Chapter 23: The Future of Growth Hacking: Trends and predictions

Growth Hacking evolves along with technological progress, changing customer needs and dynamic market development. Understanding the directions in which Growth Hacking will go allows you to develop strategies and actions that will be effective in the future. In this chapter, we will present trends and predictions about the future of Growth Hacking.

1. Artificial intelligence and machine learning

Artificial intelligence (AI) and machine learning will play an increasingly important role in Growth Hacking. AI allows you to analyze huge amounts of data and identify patterns that are not visible to the human eye. The use of AI in data analysis will allow for a better understanding of customers and the identification of gaps in markeeng strategies. Machine learning, in turn, will enable the creation of increasingly advanced and effective algorithms that will independently optimize markEng activities.

2. Personalization on an even higher level

Customers expect more and more personalization. In the future, Growth Hackers will need to deliver more and more personalized content and experiences for your customers. This means using data about customers, their behavior and preferences in order to provide them with relevant content, offers and functions. Personalization will include not only content, but also the way companies communicate with their customers and the design of products that respond to individual customer needs.

3. Increasing importance of omnichannel communication

Omnichannel is an approach to sales that integrates various communication and sales channels, creating a consistent experience for customers. In the future, Growth Hackers will have to focus more and more on creating an omnichannel strategy, combining activities in social media, e-mail markEng, content markEng or online advertising. It will also be a challenge to integrate these activities with offline communication channels, such as direct sales or traditional advertising campaigns.

4. Ethics and data privacy

In an era of growing consumer awareness about data privacy and the introduction of increasingly stringent legal regulations such as the GDPR, ethics and personal data protection will play a key role in Growth Hacking. Businesses will need to be transparent about the use of customer data and give them control over how their data is processed and used. In the future, companies will have to adapt their marketing strategies and Growth Hacking activities so as to comply with the principles of data privacy and protect the interests of customers.

5. Increasing importance of social and ecological values

More and more consumers pay attention to the social and ecological values of the companies they work with. In the future, companies will need to adapt their branding activities and Growth Hacking strategies to pay attention to these values and promote their social and ecological commitment. This can range from collaborating with non-profit organizations to promoting environmental responsibility as part of its branding activities.

6. Growing importance of micro-influencers

Micro-influencers, i.e. people who have fewer followers on social media but enjoy high trust in their niche communities, will play an increasingly important role in Growth Hacking strategies. Businesses will increasingly use micro-influencers to promote their products and services in a more authentic and trusted way. Micro-influencers will provide a valuable communication channel with potential customers, allowing you to achieve better results in terms of engagement and conversion.

The future of Growth Hacking will undoubtedly be shaped by changing trends and market needs. Growth Hackers will have to adapt their strategies and actions to meet expectations customers, using new technologies such as artificial intelligence, and paying attention to social and ecological values.

Addition

Growth Hacking Tools: An Overview

In the Growth Hacking process, it is important to use the right tools that will help you achieve your goals, such as acquiring new customers, increasing engagement or improving conversion.
In this chapter, we present an overview of the most popular and useful Growth Hacking tools that will help in the effective implementation of markeeng strategies.

1. Website traffic analysis tools

In order to optimize the website and acquire new customers, it is necessary to monitor traffic and user behavior.
Here are some popular tools for this purpose:

a) Google AnalyEcs - the most popular website traffic analysis tool, offers many functions, such as traffic analysis, user behavior, conversion or integration with other Google tools.

b) Hotjar - allows you to visualize user behavior on the website, thanks to heat maps, session recordings or form analytics.

c) Crazy Egg - offers heat maps, scrolling analysis and the ability to create A/B tests.

2. Conversion optimization tools

Effective conversion optimization requires the use of tools that will facilitate the research and testing of different variants of the website. Examples of such tools include:

a) OpEmizely - an A/B testing platform that allows you to experiment with different website variants, measure the effects and choose the best solutions.

b) Unbounce - a tool for creating and optimizing landing pages, it also offers A/B testing functions.

c) VWO (Visual Website OpEmizer) - a comprehensive tool for A/B testing, website analysis and content personalization.

3. Mark=ngu automation tools

MarkEng automation is a key element of Growth Hacking that saves time and resources. Below are examples of popular tools:

a) HubSpot - a comprehensive plaqorma for managing markeEng, sales and customer service, offers functions such as e-mail markeEng, CRM or analytics.

b) Mailchimp - a popular tool for e-mail markeEngu, it allows you to create automatic campaigns, segmentation of mailing lists and analysis of results.

c) AcEveCampaign - a plaqorma for automating markeEng, sales and customer service, offers functions such as e-mail markeEng, CRM or markeEng automaEon.

4. Social media management tools

Effectively managing your social media presence is crucial to your Growth Hacking strategy. Here are some popular tools:

a) Buffer - allows you to schedule posts, analyze results and manage multiple accounts on different social media.

b) Hootsuite - a platform for managing social media, offering functions such as scheduling posts, monitoring mentions or analyzing results.

c) Sprout Social - a comprehensive social media management tool that allows you to plan, publish, analyze and optimize content.

5. Lead generation tools

Getting leads is one of Growth Hacker's main tasks. Here are some tools to make this process easier:

a) OpEnMonster - a tool for creating lead generation forms, also enabling A/B testing and content personalization.

b) Sumo - a collection of tools to increase website traffic and lead generation, offers functions such as pop-ups, bars and forms.

c) Leadpages - a platform for creating and optimizing landing pages, also offering A/B testing and integration with other tools.

6. Competition analysis and monitoring tools

Competitive analysis is essential to gain an edge in the market. Below are some examples of tools for this purpose:

a) SEMrush - a comprehensive tool for analyzing competition in internet markEng, offers functions such as keyword analysis, website audit or link analysis.

b) Ahrefs - a tool for analyzing competition in the field of SEO, it allows you to monitor the link profile, analyze keywords or audit websites.

c) SimilarWeb - a plaqorma for analyzing competition in terms of website traffic, offers functions such as traffic analysis, traffic sources or user demographics.

Choosing the right Growth Hacking tools is crucial for the effectiveness of markEng strategies. This chapter presents an overview of popular tools that will help in website optimization, traffic analysis, lead generation and competition monitoring.
Choosing the right tools will allow you to effectively achieve your markEng and business development goals.

The most important concepts related to Growth Hacking:

1. Growth Hacking - an innovative way of thinking about markEng, aimed at quickly and effectively increasing the number of customers and the company's revenues, using various marketing strategies and techniques as well as experimentation.

2. Growth Hacker - a person who develops and implementing a Growth Hacking strategy, experimenting with various marketing and analytics tactics to achieve rapid growth in customer base and revenue.

3. Buyer Persona - a semi-fictitious profile of the ideal customer, based on the analysis of demographic data, behaviors, needs and motivations. He helps in developing effective markeeng and Growth Hacking strategies.

4. KPI (Key Performance Indicator) - a key indicator performance tool to measure the progress and effectiveness of your Growth Hacking strategy. Examples of KPIs are the number of new ones

users, growth rate or conversion rate.

5. Lead - a potential customer who has expressed interest product or service by performing a specific action, such as subscribing to a newsletter, filling out a contact form or providing contact details.

6. Conversion - the moment when a potential customer performs the desired action, e.g. purchase of a product, subscription to a newsletter or registration on a website.

7. A/B test - an experiment in which two or more versions of a website, e-mail or other markEng element are presented to different groups of users to determine which version brings better results.

8. Web analytics - collection, analysis and reporting data on website traffic in order to optimize and improve the effectiveness of markeeng and Growth Hacking strategies.

9. Landing Page - the website they reach users after clicking on an ad, link in an e-mail or other markeEng element. It is designed to encourage users to perform a specific action, such as purchase, registration or filling out a form.

10. Referral markeEng - markeEng strategy consisting in promoting products or services through referral by existing customers. Often relies on reward systems for

referral and referral customers.

11. Upselling - a sales technique aimed at increasing the value of the order by encouraging the customer to buy a more expensive product or service.

12. Cross-selling - a sales technique consisting in promoting additional products or services that are complementary to what the customer is already planning to buy, thus increasing the value of the order.

13. Loyalty programs - markeEng strategies aimed at to maintain and increase customer engagement by offering rewards and benefits for long-term use of the company's products or services.

14. E-mail markEng - markeEng technique using e-mail to promote products or services, maintain customer relations and increase engagement.

15. Social media markeEng - the use of media social networks as platforms to promote products, services and build relationships with customers.

16. Inbound markEng - markeEng strategy consisting in attracting customers by creating valuable and interesting content, instead of using traditional advertising methods.

17. Content markeEng - creating and distributing valuable, appropriate and consistent content, aimed at attracting and engaging a specific group of recipients, and consequently leading to generating revenue.

18. SEO (Search Engine OpEmizaEon) - optimization of the website in order to improve its position in organic search results, which increases its visibility and chances of acquiring new customers.

19. SEM (Search Engine MarkeEng) - markeeng strategy consisting in the promotion of a website through paid advertising in search engines, such as Google AdWords or Bing Ads.

20. RetargeEng - markeEng technique consisting in displaying advertisements to users who have previously visited the website but did not take the desired action (e.g. purchase).

21. CRO (Conversion Rate OpEmizaEon) - the process of optimizing websites and other markEng elements in order to increase the conversion rate.

22. Growth Mindset - a way of thinking based on the belief that success and development are possible through continuous learning, experimentation and adaptation to changing conditions

23. Viral markeEng - markeEng strategy in which users are encouraged to share content, product or service with

other people, leading to the rapid spread of information.

24. MVP (Minimum Viable Product) - product version z
a minimal set of features to collect user feedback and further
improve the product.

25. User onboarding - the process of introducing new users to a
product or service, aimed at providing an easy and pleasant
experience that increases the chances of long-term
customer engagement and loyalty.

26. Churn rate - customer turnover rate, measuring the
percentage of customers who left the service or stopped
using the product within a certain period of time. A low
churn rate is desirable because it indicates customer loyalty.

27. Web scraping - a technique of extracting data from pages
used to collect information about competition, market or customer
behavior, which can help develop more effective Growth
Hacking strategies.

28. Customer LifeEme Value (CLV) - the projected net value of
future revenues generated by the customer during the entire
period of cooperation with the company. Getting to know CLV
allows for more effective management of customer
relations and optimization of markeeng strategies.

29. Customer AcquisiEon Cost (CAC) - the cost of acquiring one new customer, including all marketing and sales expenses. Lowering the CAC is crucial to the effectiveness of the Growth Hacking strategy.

30. Net Promoter Score (NPS) - an indicator that measures loyalty customers to the company by asking them how likely they are to recommend the company to their friends. NPS is used as a tool to assess the quality of customer service and the effectiveness of markEng strategies.

31. SaaS (Soxware as a Service) - delivery model software where services are provided over the Internet and customers pay to access them instead of buying a software license. Many companies using Growth Hacking offer products in the SaaS model.

32. API (ApplicaEon Programming Interface) - a set of rules and protocols that allow various applications to communicate with each other. API is often used in Growth Hacking to integrate various tools and services to automate and streamline processes.

References and resources for further reading:

Holiday, R. (2014). Growth Hacker MarkeEng: A Primer on the Future of PR, MarkeEng, and AdverEsing. Porqolio.

Patel, N., & Taylor, B. (2016). Hacking Growth: How Today's Fastest Growing Companies Drive Breakout Success. Crown Business.

Ellis, S., & Brown, M. (2017). Hacking Growth: The Modern MarkeEng Mindset to Create Fast Growing Companies. Kogan Page.

Harms, R. (2018). The Growth Hacking Book: Most Guarded Growth MarkeEng Secrets The Silicon Valley Giants Don't Want You To Know. Independently published.

Mougayar, W. (2016). The Business Blockchain: Promise, PracEce, and ApplicaEon of the Next Internet Technology. Wiley.

Fitzgerald, A. (2018). The Lean Startup: How Today's Entrepreneurs Use ConEnuous InnovaEon to Create Radically Successful Businesses.

Crown Business.

Godin, S. (2008). Tribes: We Need You to Lead Us. Porqolio.

Cialdini, R. B. (2006). Influence: The Psychology of Persuasion. Harper Business.

Christensen, C. M. (2016). The Innovator's Dilemma: When New Technologies Cause Great Firms to Fail. Harvard Business Review Press.

Blank, S. (2013). The Four Steps to the Epiphany: Successful Strategies for Products That Win. K&S Ranch.

Internet resources:

GrowthHackers.com - An online community for growth hackers that offers numerous resources, discussions, cases and tools.

QuickSprout.com - a blog founded by Neil Patel, containing a lot of information on internet branding, SEO, growth hacking and entrepreneurship.

Kissmetrics.com - a blog and analytics platform offering insights into user behavior, conversions and much more.

Moz.com - A blog and SEO platform offering resources on website optimization, link building and content branding.

Ahrefs.com - SEO tool and research platform that offers a lot of data and resources for growth hackers.

Hubspot.com - MarkEngo plaqorma offering resources on inbound markEng, sales, customer service and growth hacking.

Buffer.com - A social media management tool that offers a lot of resources on social markeng and growth hacking.

Both these books and online resources will provide you with the necessary information on growth hacking.
Dear readers,

I would like to thank you very much for taking the time to read the book "Growth Hacking: How it helps you acquire new customers and keep existing ones". I am glad that I could share with you my knowledge and experience in the field of growth hacking, as well as present you with effective strategies and tools that will help you gain new customers and maintain relationships with existing ones.

I hope you will find valuable information in this book that will inspire you to experiment and innovate in your marketing efforts. Whether you are a budding entrepreneur or a seasoned professional, I hope that the strategies in this book will help you succeed in your business.

I would also like to thank all experts, authors and practitioners in the field of growth hacking, who with their work and research contributed to the development of this discipline. Without their contributions, this book would not have been possible.

Thank you again for reading this book, and I wish you success in acquiring customers, building lasting relationships, and achieving exceptional results.

Yours faithfully,

Tomasz Dmuchowski